MW00337714

PROOF

Corrections due: 11/20
Final files due: 11/22

THE MINDFUL GUIDE TO THE

Law of Attraction

THE MINDFUL GUIDE
TO THE
Law of
Attraction

Practical Meditations
to Manifest Health,
Wealth, and Love

PAIGE OLDHAM

ROCKRIDGE
PRESS

Copyright © 2020 by Rockridge Press, Emeryville, California

No part of this publication may be reproduced, stored in a retrieval system or transmitted in any form or by any means, electronic, mechanical, photocopying, recording, scanning or otherwise, except as permitted under Sections 107 or 108 of the 1976 United States Copyright Act, without the prior written permission of the Publisher. Requests to the Publisher for permission should be addressed to the Permissions Department, Rockridge Press, 6005 Shellmound Street, Suite 175, Emeryville, CA 94608.

LIMIT OF LIABILITY/DISCLAIMER OF WARRANTY: The Publisher and the author make no representations or warranties with respect to the accuracy or completeness of the contents of this work and specifically disclaim all warranties, including without limitation warranties of fitness for a particular purpose. No warranty may be created or extended by sales or promotional materials. The advice and strategies contained herein may not be suitable for every situation. This work is sold with the understanding that the Publisher is not engaged in rendering medical, legal, or other professional advice or services. If professional assistance is required, the services of a competent professional person should be sought. Neither the Publisher nor the author shall be liable for damages arising herefrom. The fact that an individual, organization or website is referred to in this work as a citation and/or potential source of further information does not mean that the author or the Publisher endorses the information the individual, organization or website may provide or recommendations they/it may make. Further, readers should be aware that Internet websites listed in this work may have changed or disappeared between when this work was written and when it is read.

For general information on our other products and services or to obtain technical support, please contact our Customer Care Department within the United States at (866) 744-2665, or outside the United States at (510) 253-0500.

Rockridge Press publishes its books in a variety of electronic and print formats. Some content that appears in print may not be available in electronic books, and vice versa.

TRADEMARKS: Rockridge Press and the Rockridge Press logo are trademarks or registered trademarks of Callisto Media Inc. and/or its affiliates, in the United States and other countries, and may not be used without written permission. All other trademarks are the property of their respective owners. Rockridge Press is not associated with any product or vendor mentioned in this book.

INTERIOR AND COVER DESIGNER: Tina Besa
ART MANAGER: Sue Bischofberger
EDITOR: Erin Nelson
PRODUCTION EDITOR: Emily Sheehan

ISBN: Print 978-1-64152-835-1 | eBook 978-1-64152-836-8

R0

Contents

Introduction

Years ago, as I was beginning my personal development journey, Rhonda Byrne released her book, *The Secret,* which illuminated a new concept for me: the law of attraction. At the same time, my journey led me toward the powerful practices of mindfulness, meditation, and gratitude after reading books by Jon Kabat-Zinn, Thich Nhat Hanh, and others. Practicing daily gratitude and meditation helped me understand the power of objectively noticing—the essence of mindfulness—to transform my life. I noticed the messages in my head and how they affected my moods and actions that then created my reality.

From my online work with mindfulness and through interaction with friends and colleagues, others began to come to me for advice on their health, career, and relationships. By combining law of attraction principles with a mindfulness practice, I could help them shift their thinking from "what I have isn't what I want" to an attitude of abundance.

In very little time, they began to see how their beliefs, thoughts, and emotional patterns could positively impact their lives. By being more mindful, they could more easily identify what they wanted, then make daily choices that supported their vision of a better future. Gratitude helped them focus on the good, which was key to bringing more of what they wanted into their lives.

The biggest secret I have learned throughout this process is that the power to change our outcomes, to find a sense of inner peace, is inside of us right now. My goal in writing this book is to give you the tools to shine a light on what has been hidden inside you, so that you can achieve what you have been seeking. Here, you will find dozens of meditations to ground the tough work of your inner practice, and in the end experience new realities in health, wealth, and matters of the heart. In these pages, you can initiate change from the inside out.

Specifically, the HEALTH section will help you define what "better health" means for you and how you can achieve it in ways that make sense in your life. Here we are reminded that being healthy is at least in part about making conscious choices and practicing daily habits that support your overall well-being.

In the WEALTH meditations and exercises, you'll first ask yourself what success means to you. Since other people's definitions of success won't make you happy, this section will help you define and locate your own path to security and abundance.

Finally, in the LOVE portion of the book, you'll become more intentional about your relationships with yourself and those around you. You will learn how to use mindfulness and meditation to observe your thoughts, feelings, and expectations—and use these tools to guide you toward more compassionate and fulfilling interactions. Ultimately, you'll combine these three sections to formulate a richer internal and more bountiful external life.

PART

I

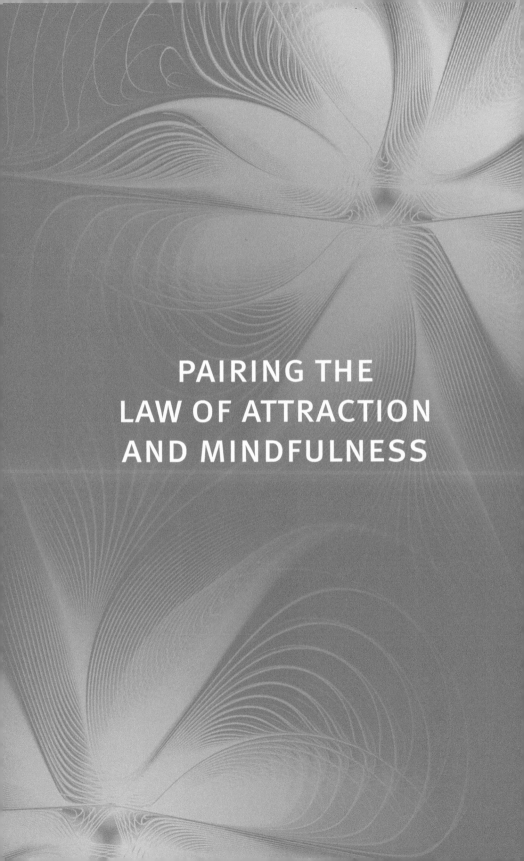

PAIRING THE
LAW OF ATTRACTION
AND MINDFULNESS

WHAT IS THE LAW OF ATTRACTION? At its core, it's a universal law that connects awareness to outcome: What we choose to focus on and believe, in turn, becomes our reality. Perhaps you have heard of "like attracts like" or "energy goes where attention flows." These are common sayings that get at the truth of this law, that where we put our attention affects the realities we experience in our everyday lives.

The discordance most of us face is that we aren't aware of our own thought patterns and habits and how these might contribute to unwanted results. Both the beauty and the challenge of the law of attraction is that it's always in a state of creation. For better and for worse, you can't turn "off" your thoughts. The question then becomes: What will you do with the awareness that they're always "on?" This is the basis of the saying (and the title of one of self-help guru Wayne Dyer's books) "Change your thoughts. Change your life."

This brings us deeper into the connection between the law of attraction and mindfulness. You might already know that mindfulness is the process of noticing without judgment. It is a moment-by-moment awareness available to everyone about what is happening within and around us, right now. And now. And now. This often goes against our habitual, lifelong patterns of judging what we see and experience. Yet, mindfulness creates openings to pause and objectively witness what *is*, without having to have an opinion or desire to change anything. It is in this witnessing that we can pause and make choices about how to give energy to the thoughts and beliefs that will serve us.

Practicing mindfulness brings awareness to negative or scattered thought patterns. By observing these habits (or rabbit holes), we can better examine the source of the life we've created. Whether conscious or subconscious, daily or a single moment, we're constantly using our minds to manifest new outcomes. Mindfulness opens the door to making the changes necessary to achieve more of what we want.

Law of Attraction: The Basics

When Byrne released *The Secret* in 2006, there was revived hype around the law of attraction. Yet the principles behind the law of attraction were there all along. People have always held the power to create what they want in their lives. Understanding these central concepts allows us to unlock the secrets behind the law of attraction and use them to create a life of love, joy, and abundance.

Harnessing your power

You may not have realized it, but you've been using the law of attraction your entire life. Whatever you have focused on with your thoughts, beliefs, and feelings has become the reality you are living today. You might say, "But this isn't what I wanted!" or "That was out of my control!"

Mindfulness can help you objectively examine your present situation to become aware of what you were focusing on in the past that might have played a role in creating your present (a deep dive into the things you *can* control). You can then apply this practice to today, examining what you are currently focusing on to better understand what your future will hold. Yesterday's actions created today's outcome. Today's actions create your future. No matter what platitude you stick to, the same principle remains: Your thoughts shape your reality.

Vibrations

We all give off vibrations, colloquially referred to as "vibes." You may meet someone and think, "I get a good vibe from them." But what exactly are these vibrations? They're energy. Everything in the universe is made up of energy at the subatomic level. The types of energy we give off are based on our thoughts and the types of energy we encourage within us.

Normally, we do not notice or pay much attention to this energy. But not only is this energy a vital force, it is also with us our whole lives. Certain emotions can instill vibrations and thought patterns that we don't desire, whereas others can instill vibrations and thought patterns that we do desire. If you vibe with someone, chances are you like how they think, how they see themselves, and how they choose to look at the world.

Identifying contrast

Most of us know what we don't want but aren't clear about what we do want. The distance between the two is contrast. It's imperative to be clear about what we do want so that we can focus our energies and visions on that to attract it. How do we begin this process?

Begin to notice what types of thoughts and activities spark positive or negative emotions in you. Then note the contrast in your emotions and physical state when you think about these different experiences. This type of awareness around your thoughts is central in clarifying what you do and do not want in your life.

Love and fear

Ultimately, all emotions can be reduced to either love or fear. Love emotions are the ones that create an open, relaxed feeling in the body: joy, happiness, contentment, pleasure, gratitude, hope. Fear-based emotions are the ones that produce feelings of tightness, pain, and closure in the body: anger, resentment, jealousy, fear, sadness, guilt. The more aware you become of the thoughts and actions that produce love, the easier it will become to invest in these ideas and experiences.

Affirmations: Pivoting from negative thoughts

If you find yourself having negative thoughts, it's possible to transform them into positive thoughts or affirmations. The following are keys to transforming negative thoughts into positive affirmations:

- » Make the affirmation short and easy to remember.
- » Start the affirmation with "I" or "My" to personalize the statement and put yourself in the driver's seat.
- » Write them in the present tense.
- » Avoid the use of terms of negation like "don't," "can't," "not," or "won't." Your subconscious ignores these and focuses on the thought after the negation.
- » Begin the affirmation with positive emotions. For example, "I am so happy and grateful now that . . ."

NEGATIVE STATEMENT	POSITIVE THOUGHT
I can't do anything right.	I do everything to the best of my ability.
I feel completely stressed out.	I'm so grateful that I've learned to use deep breathing to calm myself.

NEGATIVE STATEMENT	POSITIVE THOUGHT
Why do bad things always happen to me?	I can transform my interpretation of any situation into a positive one.
Why do I spend so much money?	I'm becoming more mindful about how I spend money.
No one will ever love me.	I love and accept myself exactly as I am.
I should have known better.	I make the best choices for myself given all the information I have available.

Power of words

The words you use in your self-talk play a powerful role in your emotions and the vibrations you emit. Positive language will help shift your vibrational energy, a vital tool in redirecting your experience. Words like "would," "should," and "could" can feel condescending and shouldn't be used (see how that works?). Also consider the Don't Principle: Whatever you put "don't" or "not" in front of, you will draw energy toward. For example, if someone asks what your dream job would be and you reply, "Not my current job," your subconscious will link "dream job" and your current job in your mind, which is the opposite of what you want.

Try to drop the negatives and focus on language that reflects and supports what you do want. As you'll see later on, this is often an exercise in self-love: "I can't do that" becomes "I believe in my power to achieve my dreams."

Universal principles

The law of attraction is considered one of a dozen universal principles. Other universal principles include the law of oneness, the law of energy, the law of correspondence, and so forth. Though these are valuable in their own right, here we'll focus on the law of attraction for its tremendous power to bring balance and harmony into our lives.

If we dive deeper, we see that the law of attraction can be examined from both spiritual and scientific perspectives to prove its efficacy. In fact, quantum physics has proven the law of attraction at quantum levels by revealing that the fundamental act of observing reality changes it, and that what appears to our eyes as seemingly solid and permanent is, in fact, vibrating in its own way.

Desire, attention, permission

It takes three core elements—desire, attention, and permission—to begin to actualize the law of attraction. More specifically, it follows these steps:

1. Identify what you desire in as much detail as possible. Visualize it and feel what it's like to already have it.

2. Focus your positive attention on achieving it. Look for opportunities that you can exploit to move you closer to your desire, and *act on them*.

3. Give yourself permission to receive it. This is where negative self-talk can prevent you from manifesting what you want. Know that you are worthy of receiving what you desire.

Gratitude

Expressing gratitude for what you already have sends positive vibrations that attract more of what you're grateful for. What you focus on grows. One of the best parts is that things don't have to change for you to feel grateful. Start where you are and express gratitude for the little things like clean water to drink, a hot shower, and a beautiful sunset.

If you can't be grateful for what you have, how can you feel good about your desire once it has been realized? For example, if you're not grateful for the money you have now, regardless of how much or how little it is, you won't be able to attract more of it. When you start to feel grateful for everything in your life, your general emotional state will shift to feelings of joy and contentment. This emits positive vibrations, helping you manifest your desire.

Loving yourself

The ultimate positive vibration comes from loving and accepting yourself exactly as you are, without needing to change or fix anything. Just as gratitude can transform your emotional state, so can loving yourself. Loving yourself as you are allows you to feel that you can receive what you desire. You are worthy. You are perfect, just as you are.

Integrating Mindfulness

Mindfulness involves slowing down enough to notice all the little things inside and around you without judgment. Though observing may seem simple, to observe without reacting requires great practice and discipline. The same goes for shifting our relationship to judgment.

As humans, it's in our nature to judge. Judging means making up a story about something or someone so that your conscious mind can categorize it and put it in its place; this happens almost automatically without bringing conscious attention to it. We judge things as "good," "bad," or "neutral." Then we tend to become attached to things that we label as "good" because we want more of them. If we decide to pursue a certain goal, it's because we perceive that the result of achieving the goal will be "good" in some way.

According to various wisdom traditions, this labeling or attachment to our desires creates suffering. These teachings instead promote nonattachment, which doesn't mean that you stop wanting the desire. It means that you're no longer attached to (or hooked by) the outcome. For example, maybe you pursue someone to create a relationship with them. You think that the relationship is the goal. If you're attached to the goal, you suffer as long as you haven't established the kind of relationship you want with the person you desire. You'll be very upset if you don't end up in a great relationship with the other person.

Yet, if you practice nonattachment, you'll be more focused on what's happening in each moment rather than how close you are to the goal. You'll pay more attention to the great times you have with the other person. You'll notice how you improve your relationship with yourself in the process. If you end up in a great relationship with the other person, it will feel more like a continuation of the wonderful present moments you experience each day. If things don't work out with the other person, you'll be grateful for all the great times you had with them and the personal growth you experienced, then move on with your life. In the land of nonattachment, there's very little suffering.

One of the benefits of mindfulness is that it can help you see your desire in a nonjudgmental way. It can help you understand the source of your desire so that you can see different ways to address it. In terms of the law of attraction, mindfulness can help you notice what you're focusing on and why you're attracting whatever it is that you're attracting. Mindfulness can help support your awareness of your thoughts and thus be a way to pause (or slow down) and make different choices around them. The following are the core principles of mindfulness that will guide the exercises to follow.

Being fully present

The term "being present" is used frequently when speaking about mindfulness, but what does it really mean? At its core, it's about being still enough in your mind and body to notice exactly what is happening in that moment without judgment. There are no narratives about the past or the future running through your mind. There are no distractions pulling your attention from what or who you're being present with. You're simply there, breathing, noticing what arises.

But what does this look like in the real world? Let's say you're having a stressful day and someone close to you wants to speak with you about something important. Not being fully present would include checking your phone, thinking about the possible negative future outcomes around your deadlines, worrying if your boss will like what you've submitted, and being very hungry while you "listen to" the other person.

Being present would include asking the person to come back after you've had something to eat, turning your phone off or putting it where you can't see it, and choosing to let go of work outcomes for now. Before the conversation, you might take a few deep breaths to clear your mind, and slowly say to yourself, "Be here now." Consider how you would feel if you were the person seeking counsel. Would you prefer to meet with a friend who is distracted or fully present?

Releasing judgment

The impulse to judge people, situations, and ourselves can be powerful. Yet, in moving from judging to observing, we can become more aware of the stories that jumpstart this judgment. For example, if you get in an argument with your loved one, you may begin to judge what they did or said, making up stories about them as a result of those judgments. The judging and storytelling get in the way of what's actually happening in the moment. When you release your judgments and objectively notice yourself and others, you create an opening for deeper understanding and peace—both internal and external.

Finding equanimity

This leads us to equanimity. Equanimity is mental calmness, feeling balanced and calm under pressure. It's a form of nonattachment and the essence of being mindful—no matter what's happening, you have the inner strength, wisdom, integrity, patience, and calm to handle it. This inner stability is undisturbed by your environment, emotions, or pain. You don't take anything personally because you know that everyone is dealing with their own challenges. It's not about you.

Equanimity means not letting your emotions get the best of you and meeting others' hostility with compassion and calm. Equanimity is knowing that it's never "us vs. them;" it's knowing that we're all in this life together.

Beginner's mind

An aspect of objectively noticing is to see things with a "beginner's mind," as if you've never seen them before. How could you see people and things differently if you hadn't already dreamt up judgments and stories about them? Beginner's mind allows you to be open to seeing what's in front of you with a fresh perspective.

By dropping your preconceived notions of how things work and what the outcomes will be, you become open to new possibilities. Instead of getting frustrated because someone isn't behaving the way you want or expect, see that person with a beginner's mind. Notice that they're human, just like you, trying to be happy in their own unique ways. See what you can learn from them. Feel compassion for them. Find gratitude for where they are.

Non-striving

The concept of non-striving can be described as, "It's about the journey, not the destination." It's much easier to attain peace if we're focused objectively on the here and now and not solely focused on what we're striving for—that thing that we think will make us happy (yet rarely does). Striving keeps us focused on what we lack and focused on the future. It creates blinders to the beauty of the present moment and blocks acceptance of who we are. To live a life of non-striving is not to give up your hopes and dreams. Instead, non-striving can help you appreciate the present in a way that naturally guides you to the place you want to go.

Acceptance

Acceptance means finding peace in the way things are—and it's very closely tied to awareness. How can we accept our current situation if we aren't aware of the abundance that's already there? The opposite of acceptance is resistance. Instead of lamenting about how things "should" be, try asking yourself how you can immerse yourself in the moment.

When you begin to notice feelings of anxiety, frustration, and anger, realize that you have a choice in how you want to respond—both internally and toward those around you. Acceptance doesn't mean apathy, naiveté, or false hope. Rather, it means dropping resistance and being open to what potential may come. It's saying, "Okay, this is the way things are. Now what am I going to do about it—and what might be the gratitude in this process?"

The Mindful Brain

Although the principles of the law of attraction and mindfulness are universal, many people have been skeptical without scientific evidence. Science, up until the last 50 years, was primarily focused on what could be measured, and things at the quantum level couldn't be seen or quantified until recently. Things like vibrations and energy fields seemed "woo-woo" until they could be tested in a lab.

However, scientists like John Wheeler, who was a colleague of Albert Einstein and Niels Bohr, have spent their lives researching and proving through quantum physics and quantum mechanics that our observations—the *fact* that we're observing something—influence what we're observing at fundamental levels. Our thoughts and the act of observing something changes it (and us) because we are inextricably linked. Science is catching up to what wisdom traditions have known for millennia.

Rethinking the healing process

Many doctors, such as the world-famous Deepak Chopra, MD, started their medical careers with Western medical training, which tends to treat the body as an amalgamation of distinct, unrelated parts that are only affected by measurable physical or physiological factors. Yet during their practice, they observed unexplainable healings that didn't follow the rules they initially learned. This led them toward mind-body medicine, which links what's going on in our minds with what's going on in our bodies and sees it all as one related whole.

In her book *Molecules of Emotion*, author Candace Pert, PhD, a research professor in the Department of Physiology and Biophysics at Georgetown University Medical Center, writes that "the chemicals inside our bodies form a dynamic information network, linking mind and body." In her now keystone book, she explains the biomolecular basis for our emotions and how they create the mind-body connection. The work of Pert and her colleagues showed that a variety of proteins known as peptides (including endorphins) were among the body's key "information substances," and each of them could affect our mind, our emotions, our immune system, our digestion, and other bodily functions simultaneously.

Bruce Lipton, PhD, a stem cell biologist and professor at the University of Wisconsin's School of Medicine and researcher at Stanford University, has written books such as *The Biology of Belief* that also shed light on the biochemical effects of the brain's functioning and how our thoughts affect all the cells in our body. He pioneered the concept of epigenetics, which states that our "genes and DNA do not control our biology; [but] instead DNA is controlled by signals from outside the cell including the energetic messages emanating from our positive and negative thoughts."

Srini Pillay, MD, assistant professor of Psychiatry at Harvard Medical School, has found in multiple studies on back pain that the physiological condition of a person's back has little to do with the types and levels of pain people experience. In one study, he found that some people with scoliosis or other spinal alignment issues experienced little to no pain while those with seemingly "healthy" backs were in severe pain. His findings conclude that, "changing your mindset and brain biology can help your brain—and lessen your pain."

Although mind-body laboratory research is still in its infancy, we are beginning to see the scientific link between our thoughts and our physical experience. Using these principles, people are using their thoughts to relieve themselves of cancer, heart disease, and a host of other ailments.

The monk's mind

To better understand the role of a long-term meditation practice on the brain, scientists such as Dr. Zoran Josipovic, a research scientist and adjunct professor at New York University, have begun to study Buddhist monks' brains. Since 2008, Josipovic has used functional magnetic resonance imaging (fMRI) to observe monks during meditation. His findings tell us a lot about the impact of meditation on a physiological level.

Dr. Josipovic told the BBC in 2011 that "meditation research, particularly in the last 10 years or so, has shown to be very promising because it points to an ability of the brain to change and optimize in a way we didn't know previously was possible." This concept, known as neuroplasticity, states that our brain can grow and rewire itself in response to new learnings or experiences. The fMRI also revealed that monks were generally more focused and could balance the extrinsic (externally focused) and intrinsic (internally focused) portions of the brain, which lead to increased feelings of "oneness" with their environment.

Benefits of meditation

Though meditation can be beneficial initially, its true impact on your overall mental and physical health grows over time and with regular practice. A variety of research has proven that a regular meditation practice can support you in the following ways:

» **PROMOTES EMOTIONAL HEALTH**

Meditators show changes in activity in areas of the brain associated with positive thinking and optimism, which has been proven to decrease levels of inflammatory chemicals that are released in response to stress. Other studies show overall decreases in depression with a regular meditation practice.

» REDUCES STRESS

Various studies have shown how meditation can not only reduce general stress levels but, by creating a neural pattern, can sustain stress reduction and thereby also reduce inflammation caused by stress. Shifting the mind from focusing on stressful situations to focusing on the breath, a body scan, or mantra helps the brain be more internally focused and calm.

» LENGTHENS ATTENTION SPAN

Meditation that focuses on one object of attention such as the breath, a candle, or a mantra has been proven to improve the strength and length of your attention span.

» IMPROVES SLEEP

Meditation can help you relax your body and mind, putting you in a more peaceful state that can help you fall asleep faster and sleep longer. It can also help you better manage the racing thoughts that can cause insomnia.

» HELPS CONTROL PAIN

Recent fMRI studies show that regular meditators have increased activity in the areas of the brain that control pain and, thus, report less sensitivity to pain. According to Fadel Zeidan, PhD, Associate Director for Research at the University of California San Diego's Center for Mindfulness, meditation helped manage chronic pain by changing the meditator's perception of pain.

» **MITIGATES CRAVINGS AND ADDICTIONS**

Meditation can improve self-awareness and help you become more mindful of your triggers, allowing you to make more supportive choices.

» **MAY DECREASE BLOOD PRESSURE**

By calming stress levels, meditation can positively impact the circulatory system thus lowering blood pressure.

Meditation and Self-Limiting Beliefs

We all carry with us a set of beliefs, most of which we obtained as young children when we were blank canvases, waiting to be painted. Depending on our circumstances and the beliefs of those close to us, we may have picked up supportive or unsupportive beliefs. Regardless of the brush strokes, our beliefs shape our views of the world and our reality.

We develop beliefs about ourselves and other people, how things are supposed to work, and how our world should be. Our mind is constantly looking for confirmation of our beliefs, which is also known as "confirmation bias," and tends to ignore things that run counter to our beliefs. But what happens when we examine and unpack the origins of our beliefs?

Though it may seem that there can be only one version of the truth or reality, there are infinite versions based on each individual's set of beliefs and experiences that confirm those beliefs in different ways. Let's take a deeper look at the "truth" behind these beliefs.

What is belief?

Beliefs are a collection of ideas, views, and opinions that you support and hold dear. They dictate your thoughts, feelings, and, ultimately, actions that deliver the outcomes you experience in your life. They filter how you see and react to the world. They're the unique pair of glasses through which you see the world. No one else can see through your glasses the same way you do. Your beliefs dictate the quality of your life.

Yet beliefs range in value. What does this mean? Beliefs can be limitless or limiting. Limitless beliefs foster growth and new understanding. A beginner's mind has a limitless view of the world where there are no preconceived notions about anything. Anything is possible. Limiting beliefs dictate that things can only be a certain, predefined way. They constrict growth to narrow pathways, fostering stagnation, resistance, and negativity.

Self-limiting beliefs are limiting beliefs we have about ourselves. They dictate what we will and will not allow ourselves to do or be. They are the blinders we wear when we consider what is possible for us. And they are often the biggest hurdle we face in our lives.

Using meditation to overcome self-limiting beliefs

Although self-limiting beliefs can be a powerful force in our subconscious, meditation affects the aspects of our mind that hold those beliefs and can help transform the limiting beliefs into limitless ones.

When we meditate, we create calm spaciousness in our mind. We have the opportunity to drop any thoughts to which we may feel an attachment, including our beliefs. We begin to put distance between "us" and our thoughts. We realize we are not our thoughts, but awareness of our thoughts. Imagine that we are sitting on a riverbank watching our thoughts pass by, like boats on the water. They come and go as they will, yet we remain sitting, watching them.

By separating ourselves from our thoughts and beliefs, we can begin to examine them objectively and question whether or not they are serving us. We may ask ourselves whether beliefs we absorbed from our parents when we were very young are representative of the types of things we would openly choose for ourselves today if we were again a blank canvas.

After using meditation to create the type of spaciousness that can dissolve the self-limiting beliefs that no longer serve us, we can also use it to consciously choose supportive, limitless beliefs that allow us to reach our full potential. We can set an intention to live by and choose to nurture thoughts and actions that support our growth. Over time, we can instill new beliefs, replacing the old self-limiting ones.

Goal setting: confidence and belief

Setting goals can be challenging when your self-limiting beliefs quietly whisper to you that you are not capable of achieving them. Even if your logical mind tells you that you should be able to achieve a goal (which is why you set it), your subconscious drives your thoughts, feelings, and actions and can have you second-guessing yourself.

If you have a goal that your self-limiting beliefs tell you that you can't meet, you likely won't take the actions required to achieve the goal or you will sabotage yourself when you get close because you don't believe you deserve the desired result. The self-limiting beliefs cast a shadow of hopelessness that prevents progress.

Using meditation to create some distance from these self-limiting beliefs, you can more easily and objectively examine the underlying reasons for not meeting your goals. You can then objectively decide what beliefs need to be changed and instill the limitless beliefs that will support you in this process. The new beliefs about yourself will also give you the confidence to take action. Without mindfulness of your thoughts, there is no space to choose the beliefs that will support your growth and change.

Making the
Most of Your Time

The goal of this book is to show you how to shine the light on what has been hidden inside of you so that you can live a life of abundance. But it won't happen overnight. Changing decades of mental, physical, and societal programming, as well as negative habits, takes time and regular practice. And there are no guaranteed results. As with any discipline, you will get out of it what you put into it. Though it may take time to notice changes, you may also feel some positive shifts right away. Beginning any mindful practice has its own energy and rewards; some are felt sooner than others.

Essentials of practice

In order to benefit from your meditation practice, you'll want to maintain the following essentials:

» **ESTABLISH A CONSISTENT TIME AND PLACE TO MEDITATE**

For any practice to take hold, it's important to create a ritual—to set aside a specific place and time to practice. For some, it might be a special part of a room with a meditation cushion first thing in the morning. For others, it might be sitting in bed before going to sleep. Choose a time and place that will support you in your practice and that you can maintain daily.

» **THERE'S NO "RIGHT" WAY TO MEDITATE**

There's no magic formula to meditate perfectly. The point of meditation is not to clear your mind of all thoughts. It is to notice your thoughts mindfully and allow them to pass without attaching yourself to them. It's okay to scratch an itch or move if you're uncomfortable. You can sit on a chair, in your bed, on the floor—or anywhere you can focus outside of the home. Practice in a way that's comfortable for you where you can maintain a focused attention.

» **EVERY DAY IS NEW AND DIFFERENT**

Release your expectations about what meditation is supposed to be or do. Every day will be different. Some days you will be more patient than others. Some days you'll have more energy than others. Be kind to yourself and accept things as they are. Celebrate the fact that you're giving yourself the gift of time and this practice each day.

» **BE OPEN TO WHATEVER ARISES**

As you begin to objectively notice your thoughts and feelings, you may feel uncomfortable. Do your best to stay with whatever comes up and observe it objectively to learn more. Seek out professional support if this becomes too overwhelming.

» **MAKE A COMMITMENT TO YOURSELF**

Choose a length of time that you can maintain consistently. If you're new to meditation, one or two minutes may seem like an eternity. Starting with as little as 30 seconds can be enough to shift your state of mind and develop a new habit of intention and awareness. If you normally practice for 15 minutes each day and one day you get restless after seven, stick with it until the full 15 minutes have passed. Learn how to work through the discomfort. Your commitment to the full time will help you commit in other areas of your life.

Keep in mind

As noted above, every day will be different. What is easy today may seem difficult tomorrow. The following best practices will help you utilize your practice as a tool for growth and abundance:

» **SET AN INTENTION**

It can be helpful to set an intention before each meditation regarding what you would like to create in your life. For example, you may begin your practice by saying, "May I find more peace" or simply, "Peace." Being specific with your intention will help you attract what you desire.

» **CHALLENGE YOURSELF**

As you develop your meditation practice, challenge yourself by lengthening the time you meditate or by changing your environment. Meditating in an area that includes distractions can help you bring your focus back to your breath, regardless of what is happening around you.

There will inevitably be times in your practice when you become frustrated. Maybe you don't think you're making progress or you're frustrated with a seeming inability to calm your mind. Frustration comes from not meeting an expectation. Use your practice to examine your expectations, see if you can release them, and accept whatever arises. You can also use the knowledge you gain from objectively observing your expectations to deepen your practice and knowledge of yourself.

» JOURNAL AFTER YOUR MEDITATION

Journaling after your meditation can help you process any thoughts or difficult emotions that may arise during your meditation. Writing them out can help you end the cycle and bring the thoughts to a resolution. Journaling can also become a record for your breakthroughs and reexamination of self-limiting beliefs.

» EXPERIMENT

Experiment with your practice. Since there's no "right" way to meditate, whatever you try can help. Experiment with the length of time that you meditate, the location, your point of focus (your breath, a mantra, a point of visual focus, etc.), and the type of meditation.

Types of meditations

Meditation can happen in many places, in many ways, and under many circumstances. Sitting cross-legged on a meditation pillow is only one way to meditate. Walking meditations allow you to slow down and notice how it feels as each part of your foot touches the floor. You could meditate while washing dishes or folding clothes, mindfully focusing on the details of each action. The point of meditation is to bring you into the present moment and increase your awareness.

Most of the meditations in this book begin with some type of breath work, or *pranayama*, as it is known in yoga. Different breathing exercises can help you relax, feel energized or focused, or simply ground yourself before meditating. Breathwork can also deter mental distractions.

Some of the meditations include a body scan, where you mentally scan your body from head to toe or vice versa, noticing whatever sensations exist in the moment. Your body can provide a wealth of information about your thoughts and feelings that will assist you throughout your mindfulness and meditation practices.

As we explore a variety of meditations in the second half of this book, they will generally fall into the following three categories:

MINDFUL THOUGHT EXERCISES

When we review things analytically, we must judge them in order to put them into categories. When we review things mindfully, we tune into our body and listen for the messages that tell us how to intuitively respond. The Thought exercises here allow you to create a quiet space where you can reflect on concepts in a mindful way. Frequently, we view thought exercises—like deciding whether to take a new job or jump into a new relationship—in an analytical way, possibly weighing pros and cons. Meditative thought exercises bring us into the present moment of our bodies. The blank pages after these meditations are literally breathing room, or a space to write down what comes up without judgment.

VISUALIZATION

Pure visualization is a form of guided imagery where you conceptualize and live (in your mind) in a future where a goal has already been realized. It allows you to see, hear, feel, and experience the emotions of a desired future. Visualization meditation employs a similar tactic, but concentrates that focus on someone or something. Using traditional and more meditative visualizations allows you to see and experience your desires more clearly and feel how the desired goals, and object of focus, affect you on a cellular level. Employing visualizations with a beginner's mind, you can begin to clarify what you desire and set intentions to focus your energy on those targets. Many professional athletes use detailed visualizations to prepare for their games. Others use visualizations to send love, peace, forgiveness, or any other concentrated feeling to someone in their life. Science has proven that visualizations impact us physically, whether we are training for a marathon or trying to heal a relationship. In a meditative state, visualizations allow us to rehearse our future life so that we are better equipped to live it when it actualizes.

INTERCONNECTEDNESS

Imagining a deep unity with others during meditation is a way to dissolve differences between ourselves and others and our environment and help us better understand our interconnectedness. These types of meditations help us see that there is no "us vs. them"—and even work to keep our own ego in check. If we're all connected, then we're all more similar than we may care to admit. What's more, our idea of the self might be less rigid than we may have always believed. These types of meditations allow us to better understand others so that we may feel compassion instead of anger or resentment. They also allow us to better understand ourselves so that we may understand what drives us, where our desires come from, and how to feel compassion for ourselves.

Definitions

BEGINNER'S MIND: To see something with fresh eyes, as if you have never seen it or experienced anything like it before. To approach something as a beginner with no preconceptions.

BEING PRESENT: Being still in your mind and body with no distractions, noticing what is happening in that moment without judgment.

CONTRAST: When examining an aspect of your life, understand specifically what you do not want so that you can be very specific about what you do want. The things you do and do not want are contrasts.

EQUANIMITY: Being present with what is without it affecting you; mental calmness, composure, and evenness of temper during periods of stress or in difficult situations.

LAW OF ATTRACTION: A universal law that states like attracts like.

MEDITATION: A technique for resting and clearing the mind to attain a state of alert consciousness that is different from the normal waking state.

MINDFULNESS: Being in the present moment and noticing without judgment.

UNIVERSAL LAW OR PRINCIPLE: A law or principle of nature that has existed since the beginning of time throughout the universe. It is the force that governs the universe and maintains balance. The law of cause and effect and the law of attraction are universal laws.

VIBRATIONS: Energy that makes up everything in the universe. Everything, including thoughts and emotions, is constantly vibrating at its own unique frequency. Each frequency of vibration attracts similar frequencies of vibrations.

PART

II

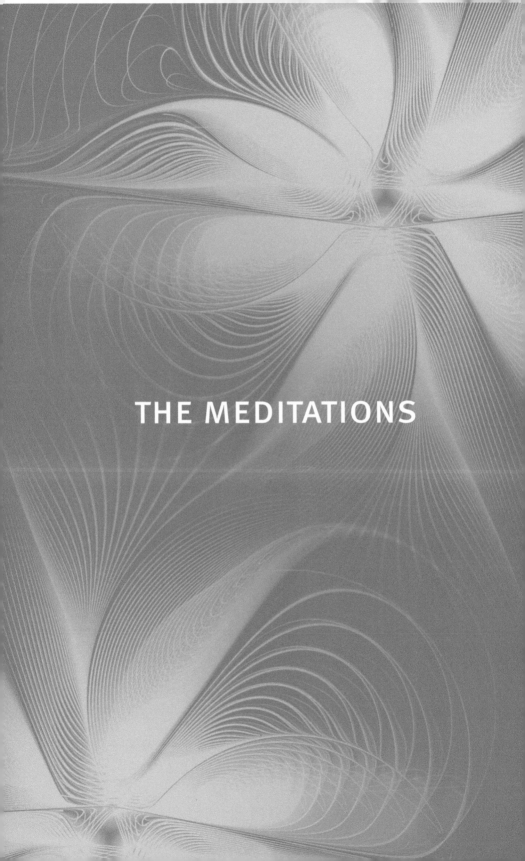

THE MEDITATIONS

Getting Started

To get started, we will begin with three foundational meditations. These meditations will help you identify the things most important to you in your life.

Why take the time to do this? People who live the most peaceful and purposeful lives tend to have their daily decisions and actions align with their core values. When your choices aren't in alignment with your values, happiness will elude you.

As you identify what grounds you at your core, it will become easier to utilize mindfulness to nurture these values.

Before we begin, it will be helpful to gather something to write with to jot down insights on the blank pages, as they arise. Flowing from your mind to the page will help you connect with your higher self.

Let's dive in.

Grounding

🕐 2 minutes

INTERCONNECTEDNESS

"In today's rush, we all think too much, seek too much, want too much, and forget about the joy of just being."
— ECKHART TOLLE

Assumptions

"There's no time to stop. I'm too busy!"

"Taking care of myself is selfish."

"People will think I'm daydreaming."

Affirmations

"Taking care of myself helps me care for others."

"Slowing down will allow me to be more effective at all that I do."

"Other people will wish that they could do what I do."

How this meditation can help me

How might it feel if you could hit the pause button in your life? This is a grounding exercise to help you disconnect from what is swirling in your mind and focus on what's happening with you right here, right now. Use this exercise as the warm-up before all the other meditations. Taking a couple of minutes to pause and breathe will help you get more from all of the meditations.

Steps

1. Sit comfortably. Close your eyes. Take a deep breath and inhale slowly and deeply for a count of four until your lungs are completely full.

2. Exhale slowly through your nose for a count of eight.

3. Take two more deep inhales and exhales with your eyes closed.

4. Pause and savor the space you just created.

5. While breathing deeply, notice any sensations in your body. Listen to your heartbeat.

6. Open your eyes and look around you. What do you see? Close up? Far away? Simply notice.

7. Spend two minutes doing this. Notice without judgment. Breathe.

Your Internal Compass

🕐 30 minutes

MINDFUL THOUGHT EXERCISE

"Your values create your internal compass that can navigate how you make decisions in your life. If you compromise your core values, you go nowhere."

—ROY T. BENNETT

Assumptions

"I have to do what is expected of me."

"No matter what my values are, I end up down the wrong path."

"What do values have to do with success?"

Affirmations

"My values are my compass in life."

"There is no 'wrong' when I am living in accordance with my values."

"Success exists in many forms and can adapt with time."

How this meditation can help me

In order to achieve your version of success and happiness, you must honor your authenticity. "Keeping up with the Joneses" might feel good for a short while, but it's living in accordance with values that mean something to *you* that will bring lasting tranquility. This written meditation will help you identify what makes you feel alive in your core. Write down your answers to the following questions without judgment or censoring yourself.

Steps

1. Sit in a quiet place where you won't be disturbed.

2. Have a way to record your thoughts.

3. What's the most important thing in the world to you? What do you value so much that it couldn't change over the course of your life? We're not talking about money, careers, the perfect partner, or anything outside of you. We're talking about who you are.

4. Whenever you think of something or someone, ask yourself, "What does that bring me?" until you can't go any deeper. That's your core value. For example, if you value your family, ask "What does that bring me?" Your answers may include love, belonging, or acceptance. Those are values. Other values are concepts like health, integrity, happiness, freedom, humor, peace, connection, commitment, community, gratitude, and passion.

5. From the list of values that you have written, identify your top three most important values.

6. Once you identify your core values, it removes a great deal of effort from the decision-making process for choices large and small. If an option doesn't support your values, there is a good chance it will eventually expire. For example, working for a paycheck at a company whose culture conflicts with your values will likely create dissonance.

7. Grant yourself permission to honor, create space for, and adhere to these values for as long as they serve you.

Energy Inventory

🕐 15 minutes

MINDFUL THOUGHT EXERCISE

---

*"The best way to capture moments is to pay attention.
This is how we cultivate mindfulness. Mindfulness means
being awake. It means knowing what you are doing."*

—JON KABAT-ZINN

Assumptions

*"Everyone has obliga-
tions that they may
not agree with."*

*"I couldn't possibly cut
anything out of my day.
It's all too important!"*

*"I'm too busy to
think about this."*

Affirmations

*"Living in accordance
with my values
brings me happiness."*

*"Time invested in myself
eventually pays off."*

*"Living in the moment
brings me a sense of ease."*

How this meditation can help me

Being able to identify positivity when you're racing through life can be
difficult. Take this time to slow down and identify where you invest your
energy day to day. This simple practice can help you see what brings you
joy and where things might be out of alignment with your core values. As
best you can, write down your answers to the following prompts without
judgment or censoring yourself.

Steps

① Sit in a quiet place where you won't be disturbed.

② Examine your life as it is. Write out everything in your average day: What do you eat? Who do you spend time with? How do you spend your money? Where do you live? Write about anything that requires an exertion of energy.

③ For each aspect of your day, describe how you feel. Can you identify where you hold this feeling in your body? What emotions arise as you consider each aspect?

④ How does each item on your list relate to your core values?

⑤ Without judgment, cross out what doesn't seem to support your values. Take note: Do the crossed-out items have any relationship to one another? Do you tend to hold emotions about these items in similar places in your body?

⑥ What small step can you take today to remove one of those crossed-out items from your list?

Health

It was not long ago that the mind-body connection was not taken seriously by the Western medical establishment. Yet, after many years of scientific research, the connection has become harder to deny. Many healthcare professionals have accepted that understanding the root thought pattern, the core dis-ease, is an important step in reducing pain and chronic symptoms. Today, mind-body treatments are a major player when it comes to healing the whole individual.

What used to be called "mindfulness" is now codified in evidence-based practices like cognitive behavioral therapy (CBT), dialectical behavioral therapy (DBT), mindfulness-based stress reduction (MBSR), and many more. These have become integral parts of the protocols to treat addiction, pain, and many other diagnoses.

Scientific studies, such as a Finnish study published in the *Proceedings of the National Academy of Sciences*, reveal powerful evidence that our thoughts and emotions manifest in our bodies. According to Mark Hyman, MD, Director of Cleveland Clinic's Center for Functional Medicine, drugs may help us deal with the symptoms of these issues, but they often cannot heal the underlying problem. Of course, this comes as little surprise to those of us for whom medication has only temporarily relieved life-long ailments. That's where our thought patterns come into play.

Slowing down and becoming more aware of our thoughts and emotions, how they manifest in our bodies, is critical to our healing. Meditation is one accessible way to do this because it helps us become more aware of our thought patterns in a nonjudgmental way. From here, we can make healthier choices about what to hold onto and what to release.

Please note that this book is not meant to address specific health conditions nor replace medical treatment. It can, however, complement the medical advice and treatment you currently receive by changing your relationship to your thoughts and how they manifest in your body.

The exercises in this chapter will introduce you to mindfulness concepts you can use to improve your own health and your role in maintaining it. These exercises and meditations will help you take responsibility for your well-being, while grounding them in centuries of study on mind-body wisdom.

What Is Healthy, Anyway?

🕐 10 minutes

VISUALIZATION

"Keeping your body healthy is an expression of gratitude to the whole cosmos—the trees, the clouds, everything."

—THICH NHAT HANH

Assumptions

"I don't have time to exercise."

"Diets never work."

"This is just the way I am."

Affirmations

"Exercise means moving my body in ways that bring me joy."

"By eating mindfully, I nourish my body."

"I love my body and its evolving form."

How this meditation can help me

In order to improve your health, it's helpful to know what 'healthy' means to you. What is your goal? What is your destination? This exercise will help you get in alignment with a version of health that is right for you.

→

←

Steps

①　Look at yourself in the mirror. Note what you love.

　　NOTE: This can be a challenging exercise. If this feels too visceral, close your eyes and try lovingly stroking your arm, leg, or any place that you feel wants love.

②　What aspects of your body and mind feel healthy? How do those aspects express themselves (i.e., a strong, healthy heart). What emotions do they elicit?

③　Close your eyes and do a brief body scan. Do you feel any pain? If so, where?

④　Ask yourself what that part of your body might be trying to say. To feel in alignment, sometimes we have to talk to—and integrate—different parts of ourselves.

⑤　Close your eyes one more time and imagine yourself expanding from your room, into the outdoors, beyond your town or city, country, continent, earth, and into the universe.

⑥　Open your eyes and take three clearing breaths.

⑦　Use this exploration of strength, pain, and expansion as a starting point for your health roadmap. The more you listen, the clearer you'll become about what "health" means for you, and how it connects to the vibrations around you.

Tapping into Ancient Wisdom

🕐 10 minutes

VISUALIZATION

"Mindfulness is simply being aware of what is happening right now without wishing it were different."

—JAMES BARAZ

Assumptions

"I'm not getting any better."

"These aches and pains are just part of getting old."

"I've always had a bad back."

Affirmations

"My body is a source of wisdom when I listen."

"My body tells me when I have emotions that I need to address."

"I can participate in my own healing."

How this meditation can help me

Our bodies have a wisdom that runs much deeper than any logic could fathom. They are constantly feeding us valuable information, frequently in the form of unease. By listening to our body's signals, we can gather clues that can lead to our own healing. Developing awareness is the first step. Buried thoughts, beliefs, and emotions create stress that presents itself in many ways—backaches, headaches, digestive issues, immune system deficiencies, chronic diseases, the list goes on. Yet tapping into our ancient source of bodily wisdom can set us on a healing path from the inside out.

→

$\leftarrow$

Steps

1. Sit in a quiet place with no distractions.

2. Start by taking ten deep breaths, counting each breath. Focus on the breath filling your lungs deeply and exhaling slowly out of your nose. Try to clear your mind of any chatter and focus on counting your inhales and exhales.

3. If your mind wanders, gently bring it back into focus. Without judgment, release the distracting thoughts and start back at one. You may have to repeat this process a few times before you finally reach ten. This will help you focus and center yourself so that you can listen to your body.

4. Slowly perform a body scan from your head, jaw, down your neck, arms, fingers, back, hips, legs, and feet.

5. What kind of sensations do you feel in each area? Be curious about the painful sensations you may be feeling. Exactly where are they in the specific muscles and joints? Don't try to make them go away, simply notice.

6. If you notice an area that's sore or tense, don't try to relieve it or place judgment on it. Trying to change the current state will only cause the discomfort to persist. You're going to make friends with it. Open up and take a good look at it.

7. Ask that part of your body what message it's trying to give you. What might it be trying to protect you from? How is it trying to help you?

8. Wait for the answer. If it doesn't immediately arise, leave space for it to arrive on its own time. This is a signal you are sending to your subconscious intelligence that it's safe to speak.

Joyful Bites

🕐 3 minutes

INTERCONNECTEDNESS

"Mindful eating is about awareness. When you eat mindfully, you slow down, pay attention to the food you're eating, and savor every bite."

—SUSAN ALBERS

Assumptions

"I don't have time to sit down to eat."

"If the food is warm, I'm good with it."

"I feel weird eating in silence."

Affirmations

"I take the time to nourish my body."

"Savoring every nuance of what I eat can help me improve my health."

"Mindfully focusing on what I eat takes my full attention."

How this meditation can help me

In our fast-paced culture, most people eat on the run, barely noticing what they put into their bodies. As such, it's easy to lose touch with the relationship between food and nourishment. We forget what food is supposed to taste like, that it is from the earth. We forget that eating nutritiously can be a source of joy. The more you can slow down and notice all aspects of what you're eating, the more you'll notice what truly nourishes both body and spirit. You might also discover a newfound joy in the kitchen.

→

←

Steps

1. Select one small piece of food from the earth.

2. Go to a quiet environment where you can focus on your food. Reserve this time solely for eating.

3. Hold the item in front of you, noticing its textures, how the light reflects on it, how it responds to the warmth of your hand.

4. Hold the item under your nose and notice its different scents.

5. Close your eyes and slowly put the item in your mouth. Roll it around in your mouth. Notice how the textures of the item feel in your mouth and the urge to quickly chew and swallow. Notice how you salivate as you anticipate tasting the item.

6. Slowly bite down on the item. See how the texture changes, for example, how the berry bursts and releases its juices, how the chocolate tastes different as it breaks apart and begins to melt, how the raisin releases natural sugars.

7. Take another 60 seconds to completely chew the item in your mouth, noticing how it changes. What happens if you try to chew it 20, 30, 50 times?

8. Consider how you can bring this mindful experience to your next meal, fully experiencing every aspect of each bite.

Energizing Breath

⏲ 3 minutes

VISUALIZATION

"Feelings come and go like clouds in a windy
sky. Conscious breathing is my anchor."

—THICH NHAT HANH

Assumptions

"My breathing is fine."

"How you breathe has nothing to do with how you feel."

"Deep breathing will make me lightheaded."

Affirmations

"Breathing deeply clears my mind."

"When everything is going wild around me, I can control my breath."

"Deep breathing energizes me."

How this meditation can help me

When we engage in shallow breathing (when we breathe primarily from the upper part of our chest), we're only using one quarter of our lung capacity. Because of this, we're not getting enough oxygen into our blood to have enough energy throughout the day. Learning to breathe deeply can energize us and calm us at the same time. Different breathing exercises can get our heart pumping or mellow us out depending on the length and frequency of the inhales and exhales. The following exercise can help you see how powerfully deep breathing can affect you. This simple exercise can also serve as an introduction to yoga, which

→

includes *pranayama* (breathing exercises), *asana* (physical exercises), and meditation.

Steps

1. Begin by standing with your feet hip-distance apart and your arms down by your sides. Ensure that you have enough room to extend your arms out beside you.

2. Close your eyes, breathe deeply into your lungs, and relax your body.

3. Now open your eyes while you slowly bring your arms up by your sides and over your head, keeping them straight. Take a deep breath in while you raise your arms.

4. Pause for a moment at the end of your inhale with your hands touching overhead.

5. Slowly bring your arms back to where you started as you slowly exhale.

6. Pause for a moment at the end of your exhale with your arms at your sides.

7. Repeat inhaling and bringing your arms up, pausing, exhaling while bringing your arms down, and pausing, 10 times. Each time, see if you can breathe in a little more air, expanding the bottom of your lungs, pushing down your diaphragm.

8. When you are done, pause for a moment to notice how you feel. Notice the effects of your deep breathing on your body, mind, and emotions.

Bringing Your Plate to the Present

⏱ 30 minutes

"Understanding our relationship to eating cultivates a lot of insights and helps us start living our highest potential."

—NATASA PANTOVIC

Assumptions

"I don't want to think about my food before I eat it."

"I eat because I'm hungry. Period."

"I have to eat everything on my plate."

Affirmations

"Food tastes better when I bring mindfulness to my meal."

"I can make healthy food choices, regardless of my time constraints."

"In paying attention to my body and mind, I am aware when I satisfy my hunger."

How this meditation can help me

Becoming mindful of how and why we consume food can unlock the door to habits that will improve health, provide more energy, and boost self-confidence. The next time you reach for something to eat or drink, pause and follow the steps of the following meditation. Take a moment to consider whether you're hungry, thirsty, or feeding some other need.

→

←

Steps

① Throughout your day today, when you feel like reaching for something to eat or drink, close your eyes and take three deep breaths.
Ask yourself what need you are satisfying.

② After four bites, pause, close your eyes, and take three deep breaths.
Notice whether you're still tasting your food.

③ Consider where the food you are eating has come from. Imagine this
food nourishing all of the cells in your body.

④ When you're done, take three deep, clearing breaths. With your eyes
closed, reflect on everything you remember about your experience.

» Did you find yourself slowing down or trying to hurry the
process?
» Reflect on the tastes and textures and anything else you
noticed.
» Tune into your body. How does your body feel after eating?

Understanding Your "Why"

🕐 30 minutes

"There are only two options regarding commitment; you're either in or you're out. There's no such thing as life in-between."

— PAT RILEY

Assumptions	Affirmations
"Change is hard."	"I'm capable of making lasting change."
"No one supports me."	"I only need my own approval to implement change."
"I don't need a reason to change."	"Knowing 'why' I want to change something keeps me energized and motivated, even when things get tough."

How this meditation can help me

Deadlines and finite goals can help us make temporary changes—for example, when you want to improve your health in preparation for an important day. Yet, in order to make lasting change that will support our long-term health, we have to become familiar with the "why" behind our goal. In other words, what is your intrinsic motivation? This exercise will help you identify the "why" that can support you through any changes you may choose to tackle.

→

←

Steps

1. Find a quiet place to focus, close your eyes, and take a few deep breaths to clear your mind and relax your body.

2. Think about the change you want to make in your health. Write down why it's important for you to make this change at this time in your life. Why are you absolutely committed to changing *now*?

3. Write down all the reasons you can imagine. Dig deep.

4. Pin the pieces of paper with your "why" on your

   » bathroom mirror
   » refrigerator
   » credit cards
   » computer monitor
   » bedside table
   » dashboard of your car

5. As you read the pieces of paper and begin to visualize your "why" throughout your day, feel the feelings associated with your "why." What does your day look like? How does this "why" impact your decisions? Doing this in small increments, even for a few seconds many times throughout your day, will help reinforce your drive, your motivation.

Greeting Resistance

🕐 5 minutes

VISUALIZATION

"Don't believe everything you think.
Thoughts are just that—thoughts."

—ALLAN LOKOS

Assumptions

"I don't like
my appearance."

"I'll never look
like that person."

"No one will love me as
long as I look like this."

Affirmations

"I am amazing
just the way I am."

"Everyone is beautiful."

"I feel good just
being me."

How this meditation can help me

To determine where you want to go, you must be aware of where you are now. After becoming aware of your thoughts, accepting yourself as you are right now is the next step in making change. If you fight, shame, or deny where you are now, you're resisting what is. As the old saying goes: What you resist, persists. Here is an example of what it can look like to accept and resist the present moment:

> *ACCEPTING:* I am feeling low energy. I'm learning about and making choices to change this.

→

←

RESISTANCE: I can't believe I feel this way. I know I should be healthier, but it takes too much time.

Which do you think will realize lasting results? As you begin this exercise, have full confidence that everything you do and everything you are is good enough.

Steps

1. Sit down, grounding yourself in a comfortable, seated position.

2. Close your eyes, take several clearing breaths, and begin a body scan from head to toe.

3. Notice the thoughts that pop into your head. Acknowledge them as thoughts, greeting and releasing each one.

4. If a self-limiting thought arises, ask yourself what makes it true. Would your partner or closest friend make that same judgment of you? Recognize your awareness of this thought. Let this awareness disempower that thought.

5. As thoughts of all variety enter your mind, replace them with the statement, "I deeply love and accept myself." Feel a blanket of love envelope you.

6. Repeat this process once a day for as long as it serves you.

7. Has your relationship to your thoughts changed?

Take a Mindful Stroll

🕐 10 to 20 minutes

INTERCONNECTEDNESS

"If the doors of perception were cleansed, everything would appear to man as it is, infinite."

—WILLIAM BLAKE

Assumptions

"I don't have time to take a walk."

"There are no safe places for me to take a walk."

"It hurts too much to walk."

Affirmations

"Taking a walk can take two or twenty minutes. Every little bit helps."

"I can enjoy the sensations of the outdoors, even if walking is not available to me."

"Walking allows me to clear my mind and feel refreshed."

How this meditation can help me

Usually, we aim to get from Point A to Point B as quickly as possible. But what are we missing when we do this? If you make the choice to carve out a little extra time to be mindful as you go from one place to the next, you can discover beauty that's always around you. This exercise will help you notice the little things, and illuminate when you are disconnected from your surroundings, lost in your thoughts. For those unable to walk, take this time to enjoy the sensations of the great outdoors. This stroll is available to everyone.

→

←

Steps

1. Commit to a time when you can go outdoors.

2. Do not wear headphones or anything else that might distract you from your surroundings.

3. Start at whatever pace is comfortable for you. Slower than your norm is usually better. Breathe deeply as you reconnect with your body and your environment.

4. Notice the colors and sounds of the leaves, the sizes and shapes of the trees, the sights and sounds of the birds. Listen for sounds that are close and far away, and observe smells and where they might be coming from. Acknowledge the temperature and how it affects you, how it feels to take each step. Acknowledge if you slouch or stand up straight with your shoulders back. Notice everything you can.

5. Feel your feet on the ground as you walk. If you are unable to touch the ground, close your eyes and feel the force of Earth's gravity stabilizing you.

6. Notice the thoughts that swim through your head. Instead of getting caught up in them, look at them from a distance as they move through your mind. Think of them as passing clouds. Do they affect you differently if you see them from this perspective?

7. Notice your breathing as it changes with different thought patterns and with different levels of activity.

8. Take a moment to reflect on how you feel at the end of this stroll. Do you notice a difference in your body?

Exploring Movement

🕐 20 to 30 minutes

INTERCONNECTEDNESS

*"When we get too caught up in the busyness of the world,
we lose connection with one another—and ourselves."*

—JACK KORNFIELD

Assumptions

"I hate to exercise."

"I don't have
time to exercise."

"I don't like gyms."

Affirmations

"Moving my body in ways
that I enjoy is fun."

"Making the time to
exercise gives me the
energy I need."

"Exercise can
happen anywhere."

How this meditation can help me

What is exercise at its core? Movement. What if we thought about exercise as less of a chore than as an opportunity to flex, pulse, and explore movement? The reality is that exercise becomes more valuable when we focus on the joy of the process. If the term "exercise" is painful for you, reframe it as moving your body in ways that you enjoy. That definition opens the door of possibility. This exercise can help you see new opportunities to inject more movement and fun into your busy days.

→

←

Steps

①　Review your schedule and book non-negotiable movement time. Try to make it a recurring appointment.

　　NOTE: It doesn't matter how much time you set aside. The important thing is to start where you are and grow from there.

②　Find a movement you love, something you can't wait to do every day. Ideas can include taking a walk (maybe with a pet or another person), gardening, yoga—maybe even flexing your hands or feet. Mix up the types of movement that are available to you if you like but remain committed to your movement time.

③　Before you move your body each day, notice your mental, emotional, and energetic states. Are you feeling scattered or focused? Emotional or grounded? Energized or sluggish?

④　As you participate in your chosen movement, notice how the states identified affect your movements and mental chatter. Notice how the thoughts and feelings pass through you as you move.

⑤　Remember that every day will be different. Some days your energy levels and mood will be high, and you'll have no problem doing something active for longer periods of time. Other days your energy will be lower. Adapt your activity daily to your energy level to keep it interesting and fun. Simply notice the differences from day to day.

⑥　After you complete your movement, pause and take a few deep breaths. Notice if your body feels different. How has your movement impacted your thoughts and emotions?

Observing Our Triggers

🕐 10 minutes

MINDFUL THOUGHT EXERCISE

"When I'm hungry, I eat what I love. When I'm bored, I do something I love. When I'm lonely, I connect with someone I love. When I feel sad, I remember that I am loved."

— MICHELLE MAY

Assumptions

"I can't control my moods."

"I act in response to my emotions."

"When something triggers me, I always react the same way."

Affirmations

"I can control my responses."

"I can change my old, unproductive habits."

"I use the 'power of the pause' to choose a more helpful response to a trigger."

How this meditation can help me

We all have seemingly preprogrammed responses to things that trigger us. When the trigger happens, our subconscious takes over. One important aspect of health is regulating strong emotions that trigger a physical response. By becoming more aware of our triggers and their emotional and physical responses, we can choose different, more supportive ones. Practice and repetition are necessary to change ingrained habits. This meditation will help you use the "power of the pause" to stop, notice, and make a different choice. Remember that mindfulness is about

→

simply noticing without judging. Here, the goal is to notice when strong emotions arise and observe them without reacting. Review the triggers in the table below and see if any of them resonate for you. If they don't, use the list to think of some of your own triggers that elicit responses you would like to change.

TRIGGER	UNHEALTHY REACTION	HEALTHY RESPONSE
Boredom (no zest for life)	Mindless consumption (eating, shopping, etc.)	Take a walk, clean, declutter mindfully
Stress (living in the past or future)	Filling time with a series of mindless activities	Sip a cup of tea, meditate, do yoga, visualize a calm place
Anger (inability to control people and circumstances)	Drinking alcohol, lashing out, burying emotions	Do a highly aerobic exercise, hit a punching bag, meditate, be in nature, journal
Socializing (need for bonding or acceptance from others)	Eating and drinking large quantities of food and drink	Play games (board games, bowling, sports, etc.), create stories, drink water
Depression (creating negative futures)	Consuming comfort foods, drinking alcohol	Exercise, volunteer, meditate, talk to friends, walk in nature

Steps

1. Consider the last time you felt triggered or noticed yourself experiencing an unhealthy reaction to a trigger. Pause with your eyes closed and take three deep breaths.

2. What thoughts are running through your head? What emotions are you feeling? What physical sensations do you feel in your body? Write them down on the following pages.

3. Consider a more supportive response. What might this look like? If you can't think of anything, simply close your eyes and breathe until you feel the intensity of your emotions begin to quiet.

4. Pause to notice the difference in your thoughts, emotions, and physical sensations when you observe the transition from trigger to quietude.

Enriching Your Kitchen

🕐 5 minutes

"Mindful eating is a way to become reacquainted
with the guidance of our internal nutritionist."

—JAN CHOZEN BAYS

Assumptions

"Nutrition is complicated."

"Eating healthy is expensive."

"Eating healthy is hard."

Affirmations

"Nutrition has the ability to enrich my life."

"High-quality food will make me feel energized and strong for long periods of time."

"It's just as easy to make healthy choices."

How this meditation can help me

Our food system has evolved in such a way that low-quality, processed foods cost much less than high-quality, simple foods. This disproportionately impacts lower-income people, and makes all of us suffer from health ailments and high medical bills. Chemicals and preservatives in these foods reduce our lasting energy and are at least in part responsible for health issues such as chronic pain, skin problems, and digestive issues. This exercise will help you bring more mindfulness to the kitchen no matter who you are, or where you live.

Steps

1. The next time you go grocery shopping, only buy fresh ingredients. Pause to consider how each item came from the earth, being nourished by the soil, sun, and rain.

2. Find a new, tasty recipe that you can prepare using your fresh ingredients.

3. As you hold each ingredient, and begin to slice and cook it, notice its texture, scent, color, and taste on its own, uncooked.

4. Close your eyes to deepen your awareness of the scents and sounds in your kitchen.

5. If you're cooking on a stove, notice the changes in how the food looks, smells, and sounds as it cooks.

6. When you put the meal on your plate, place the ingredients carefully, ensuring that the food is presented in an appealing way.

7. Pause and take three deep breaths. Consider how this experience differs from eating processed foods. How does preparing your own fresh ingredients change your thoughts about what you're eating, your emotional state, and your physical sensations before, during, and after your meal?

Welcome the Morning

🕐 2 minutes

VISUALIZATION

---

*"Each morning we are born again. What we
do today is what matters most."*

—BUDDHA

Assumptions

"I'm not a
morning person."

"I'm always running late
in the morning."

"I don't have a minute to
spare in the morning."

Affirmations

"How I get out of bed in
the morning helps set the
tone for my day."

"Welcoming the
morning helps put me
in a good mood."

"Mornings are beautiful."

How this meditation can help me

If you're anything like so many Americans, when your alarm goes off in
the morning, you either hit the snooze button or check your phone. After
this, you might pull yourself out of bed, groggy and already stressed
about the day ahead. Your intuitive self knows that there are more
pleasant ways to greet the day. But how do you get there? One trick is
to acknowledge that what you think about as you wake up can have a
lasting impact throughout the day. It can affect how you feel and how
you treat others. It can affect the outcome of things you do all day. This
exercise can help you wake up and move into the day with gratitude.

Steps

1. When you go to bed, leave your smartphone in another room or put it on airplane mode. If it serves as your alarm clock, consider investing in an inexpensive analog clock that doesn't glow.

2. When your alarm goes off, turn it off. Do not hit the snooze button.

3. Lie on your back, stretch your arms over your head with your legs long while you inhale deeply, bringing as much air as you can into your lungs. Hold this for a count of two, then exhale slowly for a count of eight.

4. Inhale while you stretch the right side of your body, stretching your right arm above your head and your right leg down at the same time. Exhale while you release your arm and leg stretch. Repeat on the left side.

5. Repeat this cycle three times while you visualize your day with everything going the way you want.

6. Repeat to yourself three times that you can handle anything that arises that day.

7. Pause and take two more deep breaths while you roll out of bed prepared for your best day ever.

Unconditional Love

⏲ 10 minutes

VISUALIZATION

"To diminish the suffering of pain, we need to make a crucial distinction between the pain of pain, and the pain we create by our thoughts about the pain. Fear, anger, guilt, loneliness, and helplessness are all mental and emotional responses that can intensify pain."

—HOWARD CUTLER

Assumptions

"My body can't tell me what's wrong. Only a doctor can."

"My emotions have nothing to do with my aches and pains."

"I can't control the pain I experience in my body."

Affirmations

"My body communicates what is necessary to help me heal."

"My emotional state has a strong influence over my physical state."

"I can control my experience over the aches and pains in my body."

How this meditation can help me

Your body is always looking out for you. This meditation will help you become better acquainted with your pain so that you may find more supportive methods of healing.

Steps

1. Sit in a quiet place with no distractions. Take three deep breaths to calm your mind and body.

2. Slowly perform a body scan where you focus your attention on one part of your body at a time, starting with the top of your head, and working down through your head, face, jaw, neck, shoulders, arms, and hands. Then move to your chest, abdomen, pelvis, hips, upper legs, knees, lower legs, ankles, feet, and toes.

3. As you focus on each area, notice if there are any aches or pains.

4. If something arises, ask the pain what message it has for you and be open to whatever comes up. Listen. You may hear things you don't want to hear. Listen anyway. Without deeply listening to understand, you'll go back to repeating the negative things you're trying to resolve.

5. Each time you receive an answer, ask again for a message to go more deeply. You'll have to peel off many layers to get to the essence of the feeling.

6. Once you feel the answer is about satisfying unconditional love, you'll know that you've gotten to the core. Feel the love coursing throughout your body. Know this love is always there to be accessed whenever you want. That love is a source of your healing.

Meditation for Pain Relief

🕐 5 minutes

VISUALIZATION

---

*"If you want to conquer the anxiety of life,
live in the moment, live in the breath."*

—AMIT RAY

Assumptions

"Painkillers are the
only thing that
will work on me."

"I don't want to
focus on my pain."

"I don't have
time to meditate."

Affirmations

"I nurture my own health."

"Accepting pain is the first
step in relieving it."

"Meditation can help me
identify the root problem."

How this meditation can help me

Many chronic pain sufferers subconsciously feel attached to "their pain." Though this may seem counterintuitive, it's one of the reasons the pain is chronic. Breath-focused meditation allows chronic pain sufferers to gain a healthy detachment from their thoughts and feelings. By accepting any thought that comes into your mind with gentle awareness and curiosity (instead of attachment), meditation can help you better recognize negative thought patterns and become less reactive. Although meditation can be deeply healing, it isn't a magic pill that you can take once or twice and have all that ails you cured. The following steps will help you begin your ongoing practice.

Steps

1. Carve out five minutes of time. Even if you have an established practice, it feels so good to take five minutes outside of the normal times you practice to sit, breathe, and be fully present.

2. In those five minutes, sit down wherever you want, close your eyes, relax your body (especially your face and jaw), and notice your breathing and any sensations in your body. Notice any sounds or smells. Notice the things you normally don't think about or try to block from your mind. Let it all in.

3. Notice all this without judgment. Everything simply "is" until you create a story about it. Don't wish away aches and pains. Get objectively curious about them.

4. When you start thinking about the past or the future or all your to-do's, just notice this inclination and kindly bring yourself back to the present. Counting your inhales and exhales can help ground you in the moment.

5. Slowly scan your body from your head to your toes, noticing any sensations that you normally ignore. Be curious about them.

6. End this meditation by taking three deep breaths, breathing in for a count of four, pausing, then breathing out for a count of eight.

7. Notice how your body feels. If you don't feel any different, that's okay. Thank your body for communicating with you and tell it you will be back to explore more.

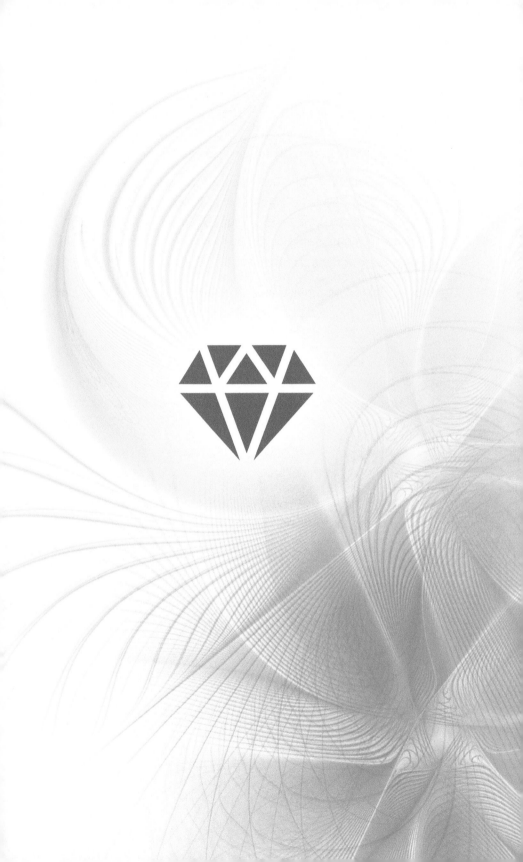

Wealth and Abundance

Monetary wealth and the concept of success are driving factors for many people in American society. Indeed, we need money to pay the bills and buy essentials, and it's great to take that hard-earned vacation or save for the future. But a life driven by consumerism rather than intrinsic desire is bound to lead to disappointment.

The reality is that many of the messages circulating throughout our society have us chasing after someone else's dream. Have you ever stopped to ask if you're chasing *your own* dreams? Can you identify them? Will money help you get there?

This section will walk you through a variety of meditations and exercises to bring awareness to your choices and the desires that drive them. In doing so, they will likely reveal how you landed in your current financial situation and what you can do to improve things going forward.

The sad truth is that most people who win the lottery or inherit a lump sum are back to where they started not long after their boost in income because they didn't take the time to analyze the underlying habits and desires that drive them.

Taking the time to better understand what "success" means for you beyond the external will expand your definition of wealth and, at the same time, foster awareness around financial patterns. Understanding the emotional drivers behind spending and saving can help satisfy those needs in more productive ways.

Since this is a book on the law of attraction and mindfulness, you won't be told how to save for the future or work from a budget. In these pages, you'll find tools to more deeply understand why other strategies may not have worked for you in the past. Here, we will shift our focus from acquiring more money to acknowledging and nurturing the areas of our lives that are already abundant. By expressing gratitude for the abundance in our lives, we focus on what we want more of in order to bring it into our lives.

From Money to Meaning

🕐 30 minutes

"The basic root of happiness lies in our minds; outer circumstances are nothing more than adverse or favorable."

—MATTHIEU RICARD

Assumptions

"I'll never be successful."

"I'll never have enough money."

"I'm not lucky with money."

Affirmations

"I determine my own success."

"My happiness is not dependent on my money."

"True success has little to do with money."

How this meditation can help me

Many people spend their lives in a job, career, or other situation that they know is wrong for them because society, their friends, or family assure them this perceived safety and security will make them happy. Then these individuals stay and wonder why they're not happy. A similar situation arises when someone is never happy with where they are, hopping from job to job or constantly negotiating their happiness with their income.

In each of these cases, the problem is that the person has not defined what "wealth" and "success" mean *for them*. Though we all have unique gifts to offer the world, if they're not actualized, it's hard to feel fulfilled, regardless of how much money we make.

$\rightarrow$

←

This meditation is designed to help you define "wealth" and "success" in ways that are meaningful for you by shifting the attention from money (the output) to meaning (the input). Here, we will look at success as a path rather than a destination and pivot from the having to the being.

Steps

1. Find a quiet place to focus and place your hands on your thighs. To energize your body and mind for this meditation, close your eyes and breathe in deeply through your nose to completely fill your lungs. Pause, then slowly release your breath.

2. Take ten more inhales, completely filling your lungs, and exhales, completely emptying your lungs, increasing the pace with each breath. For example, on the first breath, breathe in to the count of eight and out to the count of eight. On the next breath, breathe in to the count of seven and out to the count of seven and so on.

3. At the end, take three normal breaths.

4. Visualize every detailed aspect of your perfect average day. Not a "big event" day but an average day. Go through your day minute by minute. Make sure you visualize and feel what *you* love, not what you think you're supposed to do or have. Write down the answers to any question that speaks to you.

   » Where do you wake up?
   » How do you feel when you wake up?
   » Who are you with?
   » What do you do first? What about after that?
   » Where is your home? What can you see from your front and back doors? How does your home make you feel?
   » What kind of movement do you incorporate in each day? How does that make you feel?
   » What do you eat throughout the day?
   » What do you do with your time all day?

» What do you do to earn money? How does this support your values?
» Who do you spend your time with? How do those relationships make you feel?
» What do you do to unwind?
» How do you end your day?

(5) If you lived like this *every day*, would you feel successful? Would you feel wealthy? If not, what could you change?

(6) When you're happy with your vision of your entire perfect day, write it all down and put it in a prominent place or make copies to spread around.

(7) Each day, sit in a quiet place where you can focus. Take a few deep breaths and read what you have written to keep the vision in your mind. Feel what it's like to live this way. This will prompt your subconscious to find ways to make your days more like your vision.

Creating Empowering Beliefs

🕐 30 minutes

MINDFUL THOUGHT EXERCISE

"Whether you think you can or you think you can't, you're right."
— HENRY FORD

Assumptions

"I'm not worthy."

"I haven't worked hard enough."

"I don't deserve it."

Affirmations

"I am worthy of all the blessings that I receive."

"My worth is not determined by how much money I have."

"My worth is related to the value I give."

How this meditation can help me

It's important to note that there are very real systemic factors at play when it comes to compensation and equal pay. (Believing in your worth won't change prejudice policy.) Yet when it comes to achieving the level of success we desire, examining deeply held self-limiting beliefs can help us see the moments when we tend to get in our own way. This meditation will help you work through the process of changing the beliefs that have held you back. Though you may be focused on your finances, changing a self-limiting belief like "I'm not enough" will have positive ripple effects in all areas of your life.

Steps

1. Find a quiet place where you can focus. While breathing deeply through your nose, slowly scan your body from the top of your head to the tips of your toes noting any sensations that arise. Notice where you feel tightness without wishing it away. Notice where you feel relaxed.

2. Now think about your beliefs around money—income, investment, saving, and spending. Take it back to your childhood and what you picked up as a child from your parents, friends, teachers, and other adults who had an impact in your formative years. What did you repeatedly observe and hear? How did that make you feel? Write down all that you can.

3. Of all the beliefs that went through your mind, which one would have the biggest impact if you changed it tomorrow?

4. Consider why it's so important for you to change this belief, releasing any shame or judgment around the belief itself. Better understanding the "why" will help create lasting change.

5. Reframe this belief to be more inclusive, empowering, and positive. Write it down.

6. Visualize your life in detail when you've changed your old belief into the new one. What's now possible for you?

7. At the end of every day, write down one to three things, large or small, that you will do the following day to disprove the old belief, reinforce the new belief, and move you closer to the life you envision.

8. The next day, do what you wrote down the night before as soon as you can. Action is incredibly powerful. Nothing will reinforce what you're capable of more powerfully than taking action.

Pausing Before the Purchase

🕐 2 minutes

VISUALIZATION

"Mindfulness means being awake. It means knowing what you are doing."

—JON KABAT-ZINN

Assumptions

"Money slips through my fingers."

"I can't stick to budgets."

"Who has time to track where every penny goes?"

Affirmations

"Tracking my spending gives me more awareness so that I can make better decisions."

"Budgets help me focus my spending on what's most important to me."

"The more aware I am of my spending habits, the more empowered I will feel."

How this meditation can help me

If we don't know where our money goes or take a moment to consider why it is going there, it becomes that much harder to experience a different outcome. This exercise is built to help you understand the thoughts and emotions driving those purchases.

Please remember that this exercise is not about budgeting but rather about awareness. In addition to making you more aware of why money goes out, this brief exercise should inspire an appreciation for what you already have.

Steps

① During your day, every time you spend any amount of money (no amount is too small), pause.

② Before spending, close your eyes and take three deep breaths counting in for four and out for eight each time. Consider why you're making the purchase and how you feel in the moment. Remember: Release judgments. You're simply noticing.

③ Note any trends in your spending, such as when a purchase serves as a "pick-me-up" and when it feels more like sustenance. Do you tend to spend more on certain days of the week or at certain times of the day? Are there situations where you feel pressured to spend money?

④ Notice patterns as they relate to different emotional states. Do you spend more or less when you feel happy, sad, depressed, anxious, or agitated?

⑤ Notice the abundance you currently possess that allows you to support and reward yourself, regardless of the amount.

⑥ Take a moment to feel gratitude for your ability to spend money on yourself.

Values-based Spending

🕐 5 minutes

MINDFUL THOUGHT EXERCISE

"I think you will find when your death takes its toll, all the money you made will never buy back your soul."

—BOB DYLAN

Assumptions

"People with money have no values."

"I spend money on necessities and fun. That doesn't have anything to do with values."

"Money is just a means to an end."

Affirmations

"No matter how much money I have, I can be thoughtful in my purchases."

"To spend money is to invest in things that mean something to me and those I love."

"Money is a reflection of my life energy. I spend it wisely."

How this meditation can help me

Our bodies carry an internal intelligence that can help us make decisions that are in alignment with our core values. When we act in accordance with our core values, our bodies confirm that our actions are right for us by sending positive signals like a relaxed feeling in the gut or an openness in our heart or chest. When we take actions that aren't in alignment with our core values, like trying to buy happiness through things we don't value, the expenses feel hollow. Our bodies respond with an empty feeling in the gut or a compressed or tight chest. By using money to support our core values, we get more happiness and meaning from the funds we spend. This meditation can help you understand how your current expenditures may or may not be supporting your values.

Steps

1. Sit quietly with your eyes closed and take five deep, clearing breaths. Relax your face, jaw, shoulders, and back. Think about an expense you had in the past week.

2. Would you describe it as "feels good," "waste of money," or "neutral"? Check in with your body before making a decision. Do you feel a sense of relaxation ("feels good"), tension ("waste of money"), or something in the middle ("neutral")?

3. Write down your answer.

4. If you described it as a "waste of money," consider why. How in or out of alignment was it with your values? Will you make this type of expenditure going forward? If it's something you have to spend money on (i.e., insurance), are there different ways to cover that need or ways to spend less on it? Get creative. The less you spend on things in this category, the more you'll have for the fun stuff.

5. If you described it as "neutral," see if you could nudge it into one of the other two categories. Maybe the electric bill seems neutral until you look at it more broadly. If the source of your electricity is a coal plant and you're an environmentalist, it could go into the "waste of money" category and you could look into spending on alternative fuel sources. If you see the electricity that you receive as what makes all your essential tools (i.e., computer, phone, appliances, etc.) run and you couldn't do without it, maybe it could go into the "feels good" category.

$\rightarrow$

←

(6) If you described it as "feels good," did that feeling last? Sometimes something that feels good initially can create feelings of regret or guilt later, which is an indication that the expense was not in alignment with your values. Consider how it supports your core values. Why does it make you feel good? How could you spend a bit less on these types of things without detracting from its contribution to your values and happiness?

Listening to Bodily Signals

🕐 2 minutes

VISUALIZATION

"Having patience is one of the hardest things about being human. We want to do it now, and we don't want to wait. [But] sometimes we miss out on our blessing when we rush things."

—DEONTAY WILDER

Assumptions

"I need to have it now."

"Waiting won't change my mind."

"Waiting is a hassle."

Affirmations

"It's amazing how often I forget about 'critical' purchases a day or two later."

"Taking time to decide on the purchase helps me make fulfilling choices."

"If I truly want it, it will be there for me later."

How this meditation can help me

We're used to instant gratification. After all the clicking and buying, we wonder how we ended up with so much stuff we don't need or why we spent hours watching videos of our college roommate's new cat—it seemed so important in the moment.

This is another opportunity to use mindfulness to short-circuit the instant gratification process to bring intentionality to the activities that eventually lead to our long-term emotional and financial health.

→

←

Steps

① The next time you consider spending money (or scrolling), pause and take three deep breaths.

② Connect with the feelings in your body. Do you feel tension anywhere? Do you feel any resistance? Listen to the signals of your body.

③ Instead of making the purchase, tell yourself that you're going to wait 24 hours before making the decision. Take another deep breath and leave the place where the purchase would have taken place.

④ Focus again on the sensations in your body. What are you feeling?

⑤ Check in with yourself 24 hours later. Has your relationship to the item or your desire toward it changed?

⑥ Pinpoint the emotion you first felt when considering the purchase, perhaps joy or excitement. Consider three activities that elicit that same emotion.

Permission to Fill Your Life

🕐 5 minutes

MINDFUL THOUGHT EXERCISE

"There is no more profitable investment than investing in yourself. . . . It is the true way to improve yourself to be the best version of you and lets you be able to best serve those around you."

—ROY T. BENNETT

Assumptions

"It's selfish to spend money on myself."

"I can't afford ＿＿ now."

"I only want to spend money on tangible things."

Affirmations

"Everyone deserves to treat themselves."

"Spending money on mental or physical health can improve my long-term happiness."

"Working with a mentor can help me be my best for others."

How this meditation can help me

Approaching your finances in a mindful way means pausing to consider the impact of each expenditure on your immediate, midterm, and long-term goals. When you know that the latest gadget isn't going to help your long-term happiness or get you closer to your more immediate intentions, it becomes easier to avoid impulse purchases. Rather than viewing your hesitation as sacrifice, this approach becomes a way to redirect that

→

←

energy into investments that will fuel you in the long run. This exercise is about giving yourself permission to invest in the things that truly fill you.

Steps

1. The next time you're about to spend money, pause and ask yourself how this expenditure supports your values. Though this may seem like a "big" question, the goal is to help you focus on the *long-term* impacts of your choices. (All the little choices you make each day determine your future.)

2. As you get into the habit of asking these kinds of questions about small and large expenditures, you'll develop a better understanding of what truly adds to your overall happiness.

3. Give yourself permission to invest in yourself. If you have felt that spending money on an educational conference or seminar was "too expensive," consider the long-term benefits that you may derive from attending (like the ability to earn more money) that may offset the short-term expense.

4. Consider how investing in your self-care can improve your short- and long-term physical and emotional health. Write down five things in which you are considering investing. Then, write whether they will contribute to your immediate, midterm, or long-term success. (Your investment may check all of these boxes if it's truly in alignment with your core values!)

The Happiness Meditation

🕐 5 minutes

"Wealth consists not in having great possessions, but in having few wants."

— EPICTETUS

Assumptions

"Only rich people are truly happy."

"I'll be happy when I make $_____."

"True happiness is impossible to achieve."

Affirmations

"Happiness comes from within."

"Happiness is a choice."

"I can connect with my inner happiness at any time."

How this meditation can help me

Mindfulness is a wonderful tool to examine what happiness means for you. Happiness isn't some elusive, fleeting concept that only occurs when things are going as you would like. Happiness is always inside you, waiting to be noticed, usually buried under other thoughts and emotions. Another word to express this type of happiness is "contentment."

Nothing life-altering has to happen for you to start focusing on your happiness. It doesn't depend on things being a certain way or on making a specific purchase. When you find yourself focused on or attached to a certain outcome, return to this meditation to find your happiness at any time.

→

←

Steps

① Sit in a quiet place, free of distractions, and focus on your breathing as you take five deep, cleansing breaths, inhaling for a count of four and exhaling for a count of eight.

② Slowly say to yourself, "Be here now" to bring yourself fully into the present moment.

③ As you relax your body, see a warm glowing light begin to kindle in your heart. As it grows with each exhale, feel its warmth envelop you. Feel how it spreads love to everything it touches.

④ Feel the light melt away any negative emotions and thoughts. Feel it melt away any heaviness around your heart.

⑤ As you breathe, feel the light induce a sense of weightlessness throughout your body.

⑥ You and your happiness are the light. You have the ability to shed all that gets between you and your happiness at any time. Your light is always within you.

New Stories

🕐 5 minutes

VISUALIZATION

"Scarcity of self-value cannot be remedied by money, recognition, affection, attention or influence."

— GARY ZUKAV

Assumptions

"I can't afford to save."

"I can't afford to give nice gifts."

"Everything that makes me happy has a price tag."

Affirmations

"I can change my stories around money."

"Everyone can afford to be generous."

"Things that increase my happiness don't have to cost anything."

How this meditation can help me

Our financial situations are a reflection of the stories we tell ourselves about money. These stories then dictate how we engage with money. Whether it's habitual or a quick response, our actions are driven by our beliefs. Mindfulness is a tool we can use to break down this process. By becoming more aware of the stories that drive our actions, we can feel more ownership in the cycle. The following exercise focuses on slowing things down and becoming more aware of the impulses that drive behavior. The goal here is not only to reexamine your behavior but also to challenge your beliefs.

→

←

Steps

① For one day, take a moment to notice the feelings right before you commit your energetic currency (money) to a purchase. Consider such questions as the following:

  » How do I feel in my body right now?
  » Am I fulfilling a real need?
  » How will I feel about this purchase tomorrow, next week, next year?
  » Does making this purchase take me away from fulfilling other goals?
  » Can I wait to make this purchase?

② At least one time throughout the day, make a different choice than you normally would in how you spend your money. Can you make coffee at home? Put that sweater on a wish list rather than make an impulsive purchase?

  NOTE: Forming new habits can also mean giving yourself permission to spend money on yourself.

③ For necessity items, like groceries, avoid using a card or anything electronic. Only pay in cash. The idea is to reconnect you with the concept of money. Counting out bills and coins allows you to become more mindful of how much things cost and how that relates to the life energy you put forth to earn that money.

④ At the end of the day, notice if you spent less money and, if so, how much less. More importantly, notice how you feel about yourself, your beliefs about money, and your finances at the end of the day.

Aligning Values with Income

🕐 30 minutes

MINDFUL THOUGHT EXERCISE

"Don't think money does everything or you are going to end up doing everything for money."

—VOLTAIRE

Assumptions

"The job doesn't matter, as long as it pays enough."

"I can be happy doing any job."

"I can't afford to consider my values when it comes to finding a job."

Affirmations

"My work is an expression of my life purpose and values."

"I am happiest when my work aligns with my values."

"I can be flexible with the salary as long as I am living in harmony with my values."

How this meditation can help me

There are lots of reasons we find ourselves in work that don't align with our values. Perhaps the pay is too hard to refuse. If you're out of work, there can be tremendous pressure to take the first available offer. Whatever the reason, when where we invest our energy doesn't align with our values, we create unease within our mind and body. This meditation aims to help you look beyond salary, benefits, and the immediate gratification of a regular income and supports your journey toward a situation that aligns your energy with your values—as best you can, given your circumstance.

→

←

Steps

1. Sit in a quiet place with your eyes closed.

2. Take three deep breaths counting to four on the inhale, holding for two, and counting to eight on the exhale.

3. Bring your thoughts back to your values. What values do you wish will direct your life? Write them down.

4. Connect your values to your skills and passions. What do you do well that you're passionate about and that could support your values? Record these as well.

5. Visualize yourself doing these things. How does it feel to do this type of work? Does it even feel like work?

6. As you see yourself doing this work, envision where you might perform this work. What type of environment are you in? What type of people do you work with? How do these things contribute to your overall mental, physical, and emotional state?

7. Take a deep breath, breathing in all the feelings that this thought exercise has created. Allow the feelings to flow through your body. Pause and exhale knowing that this is possible for you.

Gifts of the Present

🕐 3 minutes

VISUALIZATION

"Living in the moment means letting go of the past and not waiting for the future. It means living your life consciously, aware that each moment you breathe is a gift."

— OPRAH WINFREY

Assumptions

"I'm too busy to slow down and be mindful."

"How could simply slowing down change anything?"

"If I'm physically present, I'm present."

Affirmations

"I want to savor every moment."

"Slowing down helps me awaken new experiences."

"Being present in mind and body allows me to see the beauty in every moment."

How this meditation can help me

Sometimes it can feel like if we're not busy, we're not doing something worthy. Yet when we are flooded with activity, we're everywhere but *in the present moment* where the true gifts of life reside. This meditation will help clear your mind and focus on what's happening in the present moment so that you can change your vibrations to be more open to receiving.

→

←

Steps

1. The next time you notice yourself being busy, feeling stressed out, or not able to focus, pause where you are, close your eyes, and take three deep breaths. As you breathe in, feel your lungs fill completely. Pause for two seconds at the end of your inhale. Slowly exhale for a count of eight.

2. Slowly say to yourself, "Be here now."

3. Scan your body from the top of your head to the tips of your toes, noticing any sensations. Don't judge them or wish that they would go away. Simply notice.

4. Repeat steps 1 to 3 as many times as you need to in order to calm your thoughts.

5. Take another deep breath as you open your eyes.

6. Notice every aspect of what is in front of you. What do you see, smell, feel, hear, and taste?

7. Express gratitude for something you notice. Can you identify more than one gift today?

Simple Pleasures

🕐 5 minutes

INTERCONNECTEDNESS

"The simple things are also the most extraordinary things, and only the wise can see them."

—PAULO COEHLO

Assumptions

"I never have enough."

"I lead such a dull life."

"I don't have much to be grateful for."

Affirmations

"My life is full of abundance."

"I live amidst beauty and pleasure."

"My gratitude is boundless."

How this meditation can help me

With social media and ad agencies telling us that we need to do more and have more to be more, it's difficult to feel that what we do and have is enough. It's as if the simple pleasures in life are somehow insignificant or no longer noteworthy. This usually leaves us chasing the next big thing, leaving us blind to the abundance that surrounds us. This meditation can help you slow down and notice that you are far richer than you may have thought.

←

Steps

① Find a comfortable place to sit and close your eyes.

② Energize your body by breathing in for a count of eight, feeling the coolness of the air as it passes through your nose. Pause at the end of the inhale, then exhale for a count of four, expelling all the air in your lungs.

③ Repeat this five times.

④ Express gratitude for being able to breathe freely and deeply.

⑤ Reflect on your day, reversing the time to when you woke up. Now, play the day forward in slow motion as you notice the simple pleasures that you might have missed the first time around. This might include a beautiful sunrise, the comfy bed you slept in, a hot shower, your morning beverage, greeting people who care about you, food that nourished your body, someone who smiled at you, inspiring scenery, people who might have cooked for you, or even those who watered, picked, and transported the food on your plate. The list is endless.

⑥ As you consider each of these, express gratitude for the simple pleasures in your life. This practice can help you see the abundance that is always there.

Breaking the Cycle of Material Desire

🕐 10 minutes

VISUALIZATION

"Attachment leads to suffering."

— BUDDHA

Assumptions

"If I could just have _____, I would be happy."

"I'll do whatever it takes to buy that thing."

"Everyone else has _____. I don't want to feel left out."

Affirmations

"External form does not determine happiness."

"I enjoy balancing my priorities with my desires."

"I am grateful for the richness of my spirit."

How this meditation can help me

Getting caught up in the excitement about something we feel we *must* have is easy. Our thoughts and emotions leave us hungry to fill this perceived need. With mindfulness, we can shift this cycle to bring more objective awareness to these thoughts and emotions. When we are not our thoughts or our material cravings, we become the observer who witnesses these impulses. From here, we are able to release thoughts that are not in alignment with our values. This meditation will help you see how the cycle of material desire works and how you can use awareness to navigate your response.

$\rightarrow$

←

Steps

1. Find a quiet place to focus, close your eyes, and take a few deep, clearing breaths.

2. Visualize something you want to buy. Feel the excitement and anticipation in your mind and body when you think about that thing. Feel the happiness generated by the anticipation of a brighter future.

3. Notice that your thoughts suddenly feel attached to the outcome of having that thing. Instead of feeling like you must have that thing, create distance from this thought by watching it, perhaps greeting it, "Hello, I see you, Thought."

4. Listen to the thought. What does it tell you? Can you also create distance from these additional thoughts?

5. Now, fast forward and see yourself enjoying the object of your desire. What do the thoughts tell you after some time has passed? Do you find yourself craving something else?

6. Notice how your mind starts to shift to the next shiny object and begin the cycle all over again.

7. Respond to your thought's initial desire from the perspective of already having bought it and experienced it for some time. Do you still want to make the purchase? How did distancing yourself from your thoughts and emotions change your perspective?

The Generosity Loop

🕑 10 minutes

INTERCONNECTEDNESS

"Just smiling at someone walking down the street can make the person's day. It's all about paying it forward."

—MARISKA HARGITAY

Assumptions

"I can't afford to give."

"I'm too busy to give."

"If I give, I won't have enough."

Affirmations

"I receive by giving."

"It's my purpose to share my gifts."

"Happiness is in the giving."

How this meditation can help me

When we begin to see income as energy—what we receive when we provide time and service—it becomes easier to see how financial giving can keep the energy of money flowing through our lives. If we don't give, the energy becomes stagnant, making it more difficult for us to receive. If we can't receive gifts, we also can't provide people with the gift of giving. This meditation will help you notice your perceptions around giving, receiving, and the positive cycle of money.

→

←

Steps

1. Sit in a comfortable position and close your eyes. Calm your body by taking three deep breaths. Completely fill your lungs and exhale slowly with each breath.

2. Visualize the word "giving." What thoughts and feelings does it conjure? Notice whether you label those thoughts and feelings as "positive" or "negative."

3. Reflect on the last time you gave your time, energy, or a gift. Did you receive something in return? When you earn money, you're giving your time to provide something of value to another. When you spend money, you're giving your money to another to receive something you value. Did you include these types of exchanges in your concept of "giving"?

4. Think about a recent purchase. Pause to consider all the people who were involved in getting that thing to you. Who procured the raw materials? Were there elements of nature involved? Who delivered the raw materials to the place they were assembled? Who assembled the raw materials? Consider all of the people at work. (The interconnected web of people giving their time to make your purchase possible is mind-boggling!)

5. Next, consider how you contribute to various giving webs. Which aspects bring you and others the most joy? Notice the sensations that arise in your body.

6. Consider how your acts of generosity align with your values.

Love and Relationships

It's in our nature to seek love. So, why does it sometimes seem difficult to maintain what's inherent in being human?

The paradox is that a great relationship with another person begins with the self. We can't attract the type of person we're looking for until we are comfortable with the person inside of our own flesh and bones. We have to give off the same type of vibrations that we want to attract.

Great relationships are the joining of two people who can love, honor, accept, and respect *themselves*. It's our job to feel complete and happy as we are, with or without another being, then extend this love outward.

Resistance in all kinds of relationships often has to do with attachment to an outcome when we offer this love. Even though it's impossible to control another person, to convince them to be the person we wish them to be, many people spend their whole life approaching relationships this way. Any attempt in this direction will foster anger and resentment in both parties. Our job is to fully accept and honor ourselves, just as we are, and give that same gift to others.

You'll be surprised at how much another is willing to do for you when you show your complete acceptance of them— beautiful flaws and all.

At the end of the day, building great relationships is an "inside" game, starting with lovingkindness directed inward. Mindfulness and meditation can help you hold a mirror to yourself—to observe your thoughts, feelings, and expectations. With the new perspective gained through these meditations, you'll be better equipped to start a new relationship or value your solitude. You might improve an existing connection, or mend a broken one. In all situations, the path to love begins with a good dose of kindness, patience, and—above all—acceptance of yourself and those around you.

Lovingkindness: Part I

🕐 15 minutes

"Love and kindness are never wasted.
They always make a difference."

— HELEN JAMES

Assumptions

"I don't understand lovingkindness."

"I don't have time to think about things like lovingkindness."

"It's selfish to be kind to myself."

Affirmations

"Learning more about the benefits of lovingkindness excites me."

"The practice of lovingkindness can change how I see myself and others."

"Planting the seeds of lovingkindness will help me accept myself and others."

How this meditation can help me

Lovingkindness, or *metta* meditation, sends (non-romantic) love and goodwill to ourselves and others. The ancient practice begins with sending compassionate thoughts to yourself, then layering that focus outward.

$\rightarrow$

←

Steps

1. Sit in a comfortable position with your eyes closed. Honor this act of compassion you are giving yourself.

2. Breathe deeply through your nose, noticing how the breath feels as it enters your nose, fills your lungs, pauses, and warmly flows out of your nose. Focus on your breath in this way for three more inhales and exhales.

3. When you're ready, envision someone who loves you very much, someone from your past or present who loves you unconditionally, just as you are. See that person in front of you, smiling gently, sending you their heartfelt feelings of kindness, acceptance, compassion, and love. Feel yourself surrounded by these feelings. Know that you are loved. Breathe in these feelings and be with them.

4. Now, give yourself the same loving, accepting, kind, and compassionate feelings. Say to yourself:

   » May I be filled with lovingkindness.
   » May I be safe from inner and outer dangers.
   » May I be well in body and mind.
   » May I be at ease and happy.

5. Repeat these phrases (or reword them in any way that suits you) at least ten times as you continue to feel these supportive feelings.

6. Notice the thoughts and feelings that come up in the different steps of this practice. The more you practice this meditation, notice how those thoughts and feelings shift toward yourself and others.

Lovingkindness: Part II

🕐 15 minutes

Steps

1. Sit in a comfortable position with your eyes closed. Honor this act of compassion you are giving yourself.

2. Breathe deeply through your nose, noticing how the breath feels as it enters your nose, fills your lungs, pauses, and warmly flows out of your nose. Focus on your breath in this way for three more inhales and exhales.

3. When you're ready, envision someone you love very much. Send them loving, accepting, kind, and compassionate feelings. Say to yourself:

   » May they be filled with loving kindness.
   » May they be safe from inner and outer dangers.
   » May they be well in body and mind.
   » May they be at ease and happy.

4. Repeat these phrases (or reword them in any way that suits you) at least ten times as you continue to send these supportive feelings to the object of your focus.

5. Now shift your focus to someone you feel neutral about, like an acquaintance, and repeat the sequence.

6. Shift your focus to someone who is somehow problematic for you and repeat the sequence.

   NOTE: Simply acknowledge that they are a person with goals, aspirations, difficulties, and challenges just like you.

→

←

⑦ Finally, shift your focus to a larger group—maybe people, or maybe plants, animals, or the entire Earth. Send them loving, accepting, kind, and compassionate feelings, repeating the sequence.

⑧ Notice how this practice shifts your thoughts and feelings toward the people you encounter and toward yourself.

Relationships as Mirrors

🕐 10 minutes

MINDFUL THOUGHT EXERCISE

*"Everything that irritates us about others can
lead to an understanding of ourselves."*

—CARL JUNG

Assumptions

"I don't have time to date."

"Being in a bad relationship is better than not being in a relationship at all."

"Relationships are just to get what you need from the other person."

Affirmations

"Relationships add joy and abundance to my life."

"I value myself enough to spend time with people who value me."

"In a mutually respectful relationship, we can grow as individuals and together."

How this meditation can help me

The more we can learn about ourselves and accept what we learn, the better equipped we are to nurture positive relationships. This meditation aims to surface some of the beliefs you might be holding about yourself and how they might be impacting or restricting your relationships. Understanding these beliefs can help you redirect harmful subconscious thoughts and more naturally invest in relationships of abundance.

→

←

The goal here is not to figure out what to change about another person, but to consider how to adapt your own behavior or perspective to get more of what you want or, alternatively, to decide where to redirect your energy.

Steps

1. Find a quiet place to focus and take a few deep, clearing breaths.

2. Visualize a person you spend large amounts of time with. See them sitting with you. How do you feel when you're with them? What do you enjoy talking about and doing together? Do you challenge each other or go with the flow? Begin to record these feelings in the following pages.

3. Consider your values. Do you share the same values as this person? What are their values, and how do you know?

4. Consider your energy. How do you feel when you're around this person? Do you feel relaxed or energized? Do you feel comfortable being completely yourself, or do you have to change something about yourself? When you're with this person, can you completely trust and respect them and yourself?

5. Now think about growth. Is there anything more you could learn from each other? What have you never told the other person, but wish you could? Is there a reason you don't?

6. Reflecting on your answers, is there anything you want to do differently to bring more of your honest self to the relationship?

   NOTE: It's normal for this exercise to bring up some discomfort around the person you envision. Try to release judgment around their actions and treat this mediation as an exploration of the self through this mirror.

7. Take three final, clearing breaths to bring yourself back to center.

Room for Compassion

🕐 5 minutes

INTERCONNECTEDNESS

"The ability to observe without evaluating
is the highest form of intelligence."

—JIDDU KRISHNAMURTI

Assumptions

"It's human
nature to judge."

"Having critical opinions
is just who I am."

"I'm a good judge
of character."

Affirmations

"I can see the gifts that
everyone has to offer
when I don't judge and
simply notice."

"If I'm going to make
up stories about
others, they might as
well be good ones!"

"Life is more peaceful
when I don't get attached
to my judgments."

How this meditation can help me

The essence of mindfulness is noticing without judgment. This pattern
of nonjudgment is to simply allow things to be as they are. Removing
judgment allows us to gain new understandings, to see the world with a
beginner's mind, and to grow our perceptions of what is possible.

→

←

Though it might be unrealistic to stop judging all at once, we can learn to notice the judgmental patterns that arise and begin to loosen our identification with these stories. This exercise will help you acknowledge the extent of your judgments, release them, and find acceptance of your reality.

Steps

1. Greet the day with five, deep cleansing breaths.

2. As you go through your day and interact with others, pause to notice the thoughts, emotions, and stories that pop into your mind.

3. Instead of letting your thoughts dictate how you judge the person, simply notice the thoughts and label them "thought." Allow them to drift into and out of your mind.

4. Once the thoughts have passed, see if you can notice something new about the person that you might not have noticed before. Maybe it's how they treat everyone they come into contact with, how calming their voice sounds, how delightful the way they hold their face is.

5. How does your body feel when you are open to new observations versus getting attached to judgments? Does this awareness create space for other people in your life? Embrace the room you've allowed for compassion.

Curiously Me

🕐 10 minutes

MINDFUL THOUGHT EXERCISE

"Much of spiritual life is self-acceptance, maybe all of it."
—JACK KORNFIELD

Assumptions

"I'm not enough."

"I can't believe I screwed up again."

"Anyone could do this better than me."

Affirmations

"I am enough."

"The important thing is to learn from the past."

"I accept myself no matter what."

How this meditation can help me

Self-judgment is the source of a number of unpleasant emotions and physical reactions. We do it thinking that we're protecting ourselves from the judgment of others. But when we judge ourselves, we create beliefs that begin to limit us and harm our body and spirit. The more we judge, the more we restrict. Yet the more curiosity we can bring to the inner workings of our minds, the easier it will be to bring compassion to ourselves. Using mindfulness, we can more objectively examine whether the thoughts and beliefs we've developed about ourselves are true. From here, we can be more open to positive interpretations and possibilities. In this meditation, we'll use mindfulness to transform judgment into curiosity.

→

←

Steps

1. Find a quiet place to focus and take three deep, clearing breaths.

2. As your mind settles, think about the last time you judged yourself. (There is no judgment that is too big or too small, no wrong answer here.)

3. What do you feel inside of your body when you think about that judgment? Would you cast the same judgment onto a loved one or a small child?

4. How could you reframe the judgment into an objective statement or question that doesn't conjure up emotions? For example, instead of saying, "I was silly for doing that!" try, "Hmmm, now I have more information to try something different."

5. What would a supportive friend say about the same situation? Practice saying those supportive things to yourself. This is the beginning of empathizing with yourself.

6. Be curious about the judgment. What might the judgment have been trying to accomplish? From what belief does that judgment originate?

7. Use what you've learned here to short-circuit the judgment emotion cycle and create a more supportive internal dialogue with yourself.

The Ripple Effect

🕑 5 minutes

INTERCONNECTEDNESS

---

*"A single act of kindness throws out roots in all directions,
and the roots spring up and make new trees."*

—AMELIA EARHART

Assumptions

"I'm simply reacting to
what they did to me."

"You get what you give."

"That person doesn't
deserve kindness."

Affirmations

"I'm thoughtfully responding to my environment."

"Giving is a positive
energy cycle."

"Everyone deserves
compassion."

How this meditation can help me

As we hurry through our busy days, we tend to react. Yet, there is a
big difference between reacting and responding. Reacting happens
when conscious thought is not involved, when our emotions, habits,
and subconscious desires dictate our next move. Responding happens
after pausing, becoming more intentional about our available options.
Though responding can be challenging in the face of unkindness or any
other type of unwanted behavior, there are things we can do to empower
ourselves to choose a response that aligns with our core beliefs. After
all, when we react, we lose touch with our sense of self and often later
feel a sense of shame. Compassion in the face of someone else's anger or
pain can take a heightened level of awareness. This meditation can help
strengthen that response versus react muscle.

→

←

Steps

1. Sit quietly with your hands on your thighs, palms facing up.

2. Touch your thumb to your index finger lightly. Feel the energy in the fingertips as they touch. Breathe deeply as you sense the energy move through your hands.

3. Consider the last time someone did something unkind to you. They might have cut you off in traffic or in the line at the grocery store. They might have lobbed some unkind words your way or taken the last bite of the meal you'd been saving.

4. Instead of thinking about how you can get back at them—or sending any other type of negative vibration their way—pause to consider a more thoughtful response. How could you brighten their day, calm their stress, or make the day go a little better for them? The ripple effect of your response will have positive impacts for you both, and everyone around you.

Power of the Pause

🕐 5 minutes

VISUALIZATION

---

*"Nothing ever goes away until it has taught
us what we need to know."*

— PEMA CHÖDRÖN

Assumptions

"We keep repeating the
same argument."

"If I pause, they will take
advantage of me and get
the upper hand."

"This person doesn't want
to listen to me. Why
should I listen to them?"

Affirmations

"I'm invested in find-
ing a resolution that
works for us both."

"I would rather be
happy than right."

"I care about my partner.
They deserve to be heard."

How this meditation can help me

How often have you found yourself in a disagreement with someone
close to you only to say to yourself, "Here we go again?" You would
like for things to be different, but the other person won't change. You're
both following habits that were developed years ago, the source of
which you may not even recognize. You may feel trapped.

Your biggest ally in this situation is the pause. Though the other
person might have pushed your button (yet again), you don't have
to respond in the same old way, garnering the same old reaction.

→

←

This meditation will help you develop alternative, more thoughtful responses when that old cycle rears up.

Steps

1. Sit in a peaceful environment with your eyes closed.

2. As you inhale, breathe into your heart, feeling it grow in a warm light. As you exhale, imagine this warm light spreading throughout your body. As you continue to breathe deeply, feel this warmth envelop you.

3. Visualize one of your disagreements where you repeat the same cycle of reactions without a productive resolution. Put yourself in the middle of it and feel the emotions heating up.

4. Pause.

5. Conduct a body scan from head to toe. Take five breaths in and five breaths out. What sounds do you notice around you?

6. Expand the space in your chest cavity and visualize it filling with curiosity. Ask yourself: What need is the other person trying to convey?

7. Remember to avoid judgment and the temptation to control their past reaction. Release judgment you might be carrying about their reactions and your own.

8. Try to see it objectively, as if you're an unbiased observer to the discussion. Can you articulate their needs as well as your own? Can you hold equal space for them both?

9. Over the next several days, continue to fill your chest cavity with curiosity and warm light, especially in times of conflict.

Detaching from the Outcome

🕐 10 minutes

MINDFUL THOUGHT EXERCISE

"Try to be a rainbow in someone's cloud."

—MAYA ANGELOU

Assumptions

"I'll only give if I know that the other person in the relationship is giving."

"What each person gives in a relationship should be even."

"If I give, the other person will just take advantage of me."

Affirmations

"What I bring to my relationships is more important than what I can get."

"The gift is in the giving."

"I am free when I remove expectations."

How this meditation can help me

In many relationships, giving turns into a game with a scorecard. When the score isn't even, resentment builds. But in a game like this, everyone loses. Almost everyone has deeply held beliefs around giving and what it means to give. Some only give if they think they'll get something in return. Some give but struggle to receive (or ask for help) because they don't feel worthy of receiving, hold high the value of self-reliance, or are hesitant to incur social debts or obligations. All these beliefs are attached to an expected outcome from giving.

$\rightarrow$

←

Mindfulness can help us detach from the outcome, allowing us to rejoice in the transfer of positive energy that comes from the act of giving. In this case, we give because of this energy lift, regardless of the other person's response or what we receive in return. This meditation will help you better understand your own beliefs around giving and to experiment with new ideas.

Steps

1. Sit comfortably in a quiet place with your hands on your heart. Feel your chest rise and fall with each breath. Breathe deeply for ten breaths as you connect with the warmth in your heart.

2. Recall the last time you gave something to someone or did them a favor in some way. Maybe you shared your food with someone, opened a door for them, ran an errand for them, made them a cup of coffee.

3. How did you feel when you made the choice to take that action? How did you feel when you were doing it? Can you remember any sensations in your body or thoughts that arose in your mind? Record these feelings and memories.

4. Think back to the recipient's response. Did the other person's reaction dictate your feelings and thoughts? If so, why? What sensations did this bring up in your body? Was there a lightness or tension? Record these feelings and memories.

5. Did you bring any expectations to the process of giving? If so, what were they? Write them down.

6. Does reflecting on this interaction clarify any of your beliefs around giving? If so, how might these beliefs influence your relationships? Give yourself one minute to write a response.

Finding Forgiveness

🕐 10 minutes

VISUALIZATION

"I believe forgiveness is the best form of love in any relationship. It takes a strong person to say they're sorry and an even stronger person to forgive."

—YOLANDA HADID

Assumptions

"If I forgive them, I'm letting them off the hook."

"I would be happy if they would just be the person I want them to be."

"I could never forgive such action."

Affirmations

"Forgiveness is a gift I give to myself."

"The key to happiness in a relationship is forgiveness."

"Forgiveness doesn't change what happened in the past. It allows me to release it from my future."

How this meditation can help me

As humans, we do the best we can, using the information we have at the time. Yet when others do things that hurt us, we often dream up stories around why they behaved in the way that they did. In labeling the person and their action, we often hold a grudge, carrying with us the negative emotions stirred by their actions. Forgiveness is difficult, and in some cases a long journey. Yet until we can forgive, no matter how egregious the act, we carry the heavy weight of their actions in our heart.

→

←

This same thing can happen when we harm another. We may internally acknowledge the transgression but feel too embarrassed to apologize. We beat ourselves up for what we did and carry those feelings around with us. In this case, forgiving ourselves can be challenging. This meditation can help loosen the stories you've told yourself about a transgression—yours or another's—and begin to open your heart to forgive. The meditation works by envisioning another person or yourself as the focal point of forgiveness.

Steps

1. Sit quietly with your eyes closed. Notice your breath. Bring awareness to the way each inhale and exhale fills your body.

2. Visualize someone close to you that you would like to forgive. See them clearly in your mind's eye.

3. Notice the thoughts and feelings that arise as you think about them. Pause to create distance from your thoughts while holding space for emotions that arise.

4. As best you can, free yourself from explanations of their behavior or judgments around your role. What does it look like to hold them as an objective being you cannot change, to create space between you and their actions?

5. As you are ready, begin to let forgiveness seep into that space. Use their name as you say, "I forgive you, X. I forgive you for what you did, whether or not it was intentional."

6. Repeat this five times.

7. Take ten deep breaths, in for a count of four and out for a count of eight, to release any unpleasant thoughts and emotions.

8. Open your heart, sending love to yourself for this brave act of forgiveness.

9. Notice how your body feels after this release.

Holding Space for Love

🕐 15 minutes

MINDFUL THOUGHT EXERCISE

"Peace comes from within. Do not seek it without."
— BUDDHA

Assumptions

"I need someone else to make me happy."

"Doesn't everyone want the same thing in a relationship?"

"I can change them."

Affirmations

"Self-love is the foundation of abundance."

"Being specific yet flexible will allow me to find the right partner for me."

"I am worthy of the love I receive."

How this meditation can help me

A key to the law of attraction is to visualize in detail what you want to manifest and feel what it's like to exist in this space. As we discovered in earlier meditations, we need to precisely define what we're seeking in order for our subconscious and our intuition to meet us there. In this meditation, we'll move that focus to our relationships. By defining what we're looking for from a relationship (and clarifying what we don't want), we begin to understand ourselves better. By understanding ourselves better, we can notice how we contribute to our relationships. Through the lens of mindfulness, we can see how we can create the relationship we're seeking.

→

←

Steps

1. Find a quiet place to focus and take a few deep, clearing breaths.

2. Focus your attention on your heart. Feel it swelling with love. Feel the warmth spread throughout your body and fill the room.

3. Take three deep breaths as you embrace this warmth.

4. Holding those feelings, visualize your ideal relationship. When you're with your ideal partner, how do you feel? What thoughts and emotions arise? How does this feel throughout your body? Make notes.

5. Without holding onto any specific physical features, consider what your partner's energy feels like. How do they speak to you? What kinds of things do you enjoy doing together? What kinds of things do you talk about and share? Make notes.

6. Most importantly, what are their values? How do they express those values? How do their values mesh with yours? Make notes.

7. See this person wrapped in the warm, loving light that you created. Envision accepting them completely, even when you learn about their imperfections.

8. Hold the feelings generated by your interaction with your partner in your heart as you take five deep, clearing breaths.

Practicing Patience

🕑 2 minutes

"Each life is made up of mistakes and learning, waiting and growing, practicing patience and being persistent."

— BILLY GRAHAM

Assumptions

"I'm not a patient person."

"I don't have time to be patient."

"Things will work themselves out."

Affirmations

"Patience allows me to learn and understand."

"Patience allows me to act with compassion."

"Patience makes me a stronger person."

How this meditation can help me

Patience is a skill that can't be practiced when everything is going as we would like. We need to take advantage of the challenging opportunities that are presented to us in order to practice patience. We can turn those frustrating situations into opportunities to slow down and notice the details that normally pass us by. This meditation will help you lower your racing heartbeat when a waiting opportunity presents itself and shift the focus from control to the practice of patience. For best results, read through the exercise and try to memorize it, so you have it at your disposal when out in the real world.

→

←

Steps

① The next time you find yourself waiting and feeling impatient, close your eyes, inhale deeply, and hold the inhale for three long seconds.

② Breathe out through your nose to a count of eight, all the way into your belly, and hold for two seconds.

③ Repeat.

④ Open your eyes and look around you. If there are people around you, notice their facial expressions. Linger on the people experiencing joy. Take note of the weather, the temperature, and how it feels on your face. If you're inside, notice objects on tables or walls that you hadn't noticed before. Does anything bring back good memories?

⑤ Notice the new, positive sensations in your body. After the breathing exercise, did your heart rate calm down?

⑥ Notice any thoughts and emotions flowing through you and how they shifted as you moved from waiting impatiently to mindfully noticing while you wait.

⑦ Take one more deep, cleansing breath and feel the benefits of your practice.

Give a Compliment

🕐 1 minute

INTERCONNECTEDNESS

"You have to love yourself or you'll never be able to accept compliments from anyone."

—DEAN WAREHAM

Assumptions

"People will think I'm trying to get something if I give them a compliment."

"I can't find anything to compliment that person on."

"What's the point of giving a compliment?"

Affirmations

"Giving an honest compliment, and expecting nothing in return is a wonderful act of kindness."

"Everyone has something wonderful about them."

"The joy of the compliment is in the giving."

How this meditation can help me

We feel good when we receive compliments—but why? Research in neuroscience shows that receiving a sincere compliment activates the areas in our brain that are responsible for decision making and reward-related behavior. It also releases the neurotransmitter dopamine, associated with motivation, focus, and positivity. Beyond the neuropsychological effects, compliments benefit the person giving the compliment, as well as the person receiving it. Though there are definitely limitations as to when

$\rightarrow$

←

it's okay to enter someone's personal space with kind words, in the right moment this practice can help you slow down, notice the people around you, and respectfully gift them with your kindness.

Steps

① Notice the people who cross your path throughout the day.

② Wherever possible (and safe), look people in the eye, smile, and say, "Hello." You may be met with averted eyes or an equally open "Hello!" The key? The other person's response doesn't matter.

③ Pause and take a deep breath to ground and center yourself before offering a compliment.

④ If you notice something about a person that warrants a genuine compliment, tell them. Again, you're not looking for any kind of response. You're simply giving the gift of the compliment.

⑤ Be sure to practice these concepts with new acquaintances as well as people close to you. If loved ones aren't used to receiving compliments from you, they may be pleasantly surprised.

⑥ At the end of your day, sit in a quiet place, close your eyes, and take a few deep breaths.

⑦ Reflect on your experience of acknowledging others and how those experiences might have shifted your feelings about yourself and energy toward others. You never know when one of those interactions might lead to a deep and lasting relationship.

Mindful Listening

🕐 5 minutes

INTERCONNECTEDNESS

"Seek first to understand, then to be understood."
—STEPHEN R. COVEY

Assumptions

"I won't have a good response if I'm not thinking about it while the other person is talking."

"I'm just trying to get my message across."

"Why should I listen to them if they're not going to listen to me?"

Affirmations

"I can learn much more by listening than from speaking."

"We all simply want to be heard."

"Slowing down to truly listen conveys to the other person how important they are to me."

How this meditation can help me

The "pregnant pause"—that lull in a conversation when no one says anything—can feel uncomfortable. To avoid it, many fill the space with opinions or ideas. Often, we're more interested in reaffirming our own point than learning more about the other person. In these cases, there's no true connection, often leaving both parties to feel misunderstood. Yet, when both people embrace the pause, it leaves room to create thoughtfulness and greater understanding, changing the outcome of the conversation. In this exercise, we'll experiment with mindfully listening

→

←

to another. By allowing the other person to feel heard, you can open the door to a deeper connection and greater commitment to one another.

Tip: When beginning this exercise, you may want to set a timer to allow each person an equal and agreed upon amount of time to speak. This can impose mindful listening.

Steps

1. The next time you have a conversation with your partner or someone close to you, focus your attention on that person completely. Put away your phone and any other distractions. Take a few deep, clearing breaths to become fully present.

2. Look into their eyes when they speak. In addition to listening to what they're saying, see if you can pick up on their emotional state.

3. As they're speaking, notice the thoughts and emotions going through your mind. Are you formulating your response? Are you judging what they're saying? Is what they're saying conjuring up any type of emotion for you?

4. Each time you notice a thought, use it as a cue to refocus your attention on what the other person is saying. Seek to fully understand what they're trying to communicate.

5. When you would normally begin speaking, instead, embrace the pause with a deep breath through the nose, releasing it slowly through your mouth. Use the space to actively listen. Linger longer than you normally would when they stop speaking.

6. Once you are certain they are finished speaking, reflect on what you heard to ensure that you've understood their needs. Ask clarifying questions. Ask them if they feel you've been an active listener.

7. Practice this mindful listening as often as you can, and see how it changes your relationships.

Mindful Speaking

🕑 5 minutes

INTERCONNECTEDNESS

"The little things? The little moments? They aren't little."
— JON KABAT-ZINN

Assumptions

"Everyone should understand what I say."

"I don't leave anything open to interpretation."

"They know what I'm talking about."

Affirmations

"It's important to understand my audience before I speak."

"Everyone hears the same words uniquely."

"Pausing to consider how my words and body language might be interpreted is critical to being understood."

How this meditation can help me

It's important to remember that everyone sees and hears the world through the filter of their own beliefs, past experiences, and current emotional state. As such, it's advantageous for everyone if we pause and consider how we can effectively deliver our message so that the other person receives it as we intend. This practice uses mindfulness to communicate more effectively.

$\rightarrow$

$\leftarrow$

Steps

1. Set aside time to talk to a loved one. Be intentional about this date.

2. Let them speak first and allow yourself to be fully present. Put away your phone and any other potential distractions. Simply be there for them.

3. Listen to the words they're saying. Notice their body language. Notice their emotional and energetic state. Are they communicating more than what their words are saying?

4. When the conversation shifts to you, before you respond, ensure that you have heard and correctly understood what the other person said by reflecting your understanding to them.

5. After you receive confirmation from the other person that you heard them correctly, take a deep, clearing breath to center yourself.

6. Pause to carefully consider the most effective way to convey what you want to say, given the other person's current state. Consider your words, tone, body language, and environment. Challenge yourself to see how supportive you can be as you convey that message.

7. After you have spoken, notice the other person's response without reacting to this response. You are simply observing. Do their words, tone, and body language convey their understanding? Did your message change their emotional state? If so, was it in a desired or undesired way?

8. After the conversation, take note: Does the other person seem more receptive to your messages? What sensations do you feel in your body? What emotions do you feel?

   NOTE: How can you use what you learned to shift future conversations so that both parties feel understood?

In Conclusion

Being mindful that the law of attraction never rests was the first part of your journey. With this book in your hands, you arrived. The next step was committing to the work of awareness— examining the thought patterns and behaviors that dictate your present and future.

In my experience, the single most effective way to sustain this process is to express daily gratitude. This can be through meditations such as the ones presented here or an alternative ritual that grounds you to the present. Simply writing down at least three things you're grateful for each day, feeling the gratitude, and not repeating what you've written on previous days will rewire your brain (thank you, neuroplasticity!) to focus on the abundance in your life—and draw more of it toward you.

Meditating on your gratitude list each day will help reinforce the positive vibrations. What's more, just knowing that you'll be writing your gratitude list at the same time each day will activate your subconscious to always be on the lookout for what you'll write next time. Throughout the day, you'll be looking for the next special thing to add. This is also a powerful antidote against depression and anxiety.

As with any new practice, start small; take baby steps. Make a commitment to yourself to engage with these practices daily. The changes may not be noticeable at first, but they will build over time. In the near future, you will pause to reflect on how far you have come. The universe will take it from there.

Further Reading

Mindfulness

Hoff, Benjamin. *The Tao of Pooh*. New York: Penguin Books, 1982.

Kabat-Zinn, Jon. *Mindfulness for Beginners: Reclaiming the Present Moment—and Your Life*. Louisville, CO: Sounds True, 2016.

Kabat-Zinn, Jon. *Wherever You Go, There You Are: Mindfulness Meditation in Everyday Life*. New York: Hachette Books, 2005.

Nhat Hanh, Thich. *Being Peace*. Berkeley, CA: Parallax Press, 1996.

Law of Attraction

Arntz, William, Betsy Chasse, and Mark Vicente. *What the Bleep Do We Know!?™: Discovering the Endless Possibilities for Altering Your Everyday Reality*. Deerfield Beach, FL: Health Communications Inc., 2007.

Byrne, Rhonda. *The Secret*. New York: Atria Books/Beyond Words, 2006.

Gallagher, Victoria. *Practical Law of Attraction: Align Yourself with the Manifesting Conditions and Successfully Attract Your Desires*. Independently published, 2019.

Health

Chopra, Deepak. *Reinventing the Body, Resurrecting the Soul: How to Create a New You*. New York: Harmony, 2010.

Lipton, Bruce H. *The Biology of Belief: Unleashing the Power of Consciousness, Matter, and Miracles*. Carlsbad, CA.: Hay House, Inc., 2008.

Lipton, Bruce H., and Steve Bhaerman. *Spontaneous Evolution: Our Positive Future (and a Way to Get There from Here)*. Carlsbad, CA: Hay House, Inc., 2009.

Pert, Candace B. *Molecules of Emotion: The Science Behind Mind-Body Medicine*. New York: Touchstone, CA: 1999.

Money and Abundance

Dominguez, Joe, and Vicki Robin. *Your Money or Your Life: Transforming Your Relationship with Money and Achieving Financial Independence*. New York: Penguin Books, 1992.

Franklin, Bryan, and Michael Ellsberg. *The Last Safe Investment: Spending Now to Increase Your True Wealth Forever*. New York: Portfolio/Penguin, 2016.

Tessler, Bari. *The Art of Money: A Life-Changing Guide to Financial Happiness*. Berkeley, CA.: Parallax Press, 2016.

Love and Relationships

Davenport, Barrie. *201 Relationship Questions: The Couple's Guide to Building Trust and Emotional Intimacy*. Independently published, 2015.

Hendricks, Gay. *Learning to Love Yourself*. Independently published, 2011.

Richo, David. *How to Be an Adult in Relationships: The Five Keys to Mindful Loving*. Boulder, CO: Shambhala, 2002.

Walser, Robyn D., and Darrah Westrup. *The Mindful Couple: How Acceptance and Mindfulness Can Lead You to the Love You Want*. Oakland, CA: New Harbinger Publications, Inc., 2009.

Index

About the Author

 **PAIGE OLDHAM** spent years defining herself as a financial executive in corporate America. She understands that we need to find more effective ways of achieving our versions of happiness and success. The traditional methodologies are no longer working for us. In fact, they're making us more stressed and less happy by the day. Now she follows her heart and has expanded her joy as a wife, mother, writer, mindfulness expert, and yogini in the mountains outside of Colorado Springs, Colorado. Nurturing positivity through mindfulness, she is living her dream life. You can find more of her writings at SimpleMindfulness.com.